YOUR HORSE'S
Skin

The author with Mabel.

HILARY POOLEY
YOUR HORSE'S
Skin

J.A. ALLEN · LONDON

© Hilary Pooley 2005
First published in Great Britain in 2005

ISBN 0 85131 883 5

J. A. Allen
Clerkenwell House
Clerkenwell Green
London ECIR OHT

J. A. Allen is an imprint of Robert Hale Limited

British Library Cataloguing in Publication Data
A catalogue record for this book is available from the British Library

Edited by John Beaton
Design and typesetting by Paul Saunders

Colour separation by Tenon & Polert Colour Scanning Limited, Hong Kong
Printed in China by New Era Printing Company Ltd

To my son Alex and to Carol and Olivier Faith –
all of whom kept me at it

Contents

Introduction

For what is life so full of care we have no time to stand and stare.

Owning and looking after horses can be a fascinating and rewarding occupation either as a hobby or, for some lucky few, a lifelong obsession and career. However our equine friends can be delicate creatures and many things can and do go wrong. Keeping a horse requires meticulous attention to detail if they are to remain healthy and happy.

Proper nutrition and a suitable environment with fresh air and exercise are of prime importance in maintaining a healthy, happy equine but some of the most useful tools available to assist us in this endeavour are our own senses of sight, touch, smell and hearing.

Time spent observing a horse in his stable and out in the field, watching the way he moves and noting his natural body rhythms, is never wasted. Similarly learning what the horse in health feels like under the hand is of equal importance and being able to interpret what visual observation and the sense of touch can reveal is one of the greatest skills a horse owner can develop.

When we look at a horse what we see before anything else, apart from his shape and demeanour, is his coat. At a glance the experienced horseman (or woman) will assimilate information upon which to base a judgment about the animal. Whether the hair is coarse or fine, glossy or dull, whether it is long and shaggy or short and close and whether it is flat or staring. From this information can be deduced, not only how the horse is bred and what type of equine his ancestors were, but also a great deal about his state of general health and psychological well-being. There is no trick to this and it is a valuable skill that

Mabel, grazing peacefully in the early morning.

all horse owners can acquire, that is if we know what we are looking at and take the time to practise!

In addition to our powers of observation our sense of touch also provides information with which to evaluate the condition of a horse. Is he hot or cold to the touch, is his skin dry and tight or loose and supple, does his coat feel dirty and sticky and importantly, when we touch him, is there any evidence of pain?

Lastly but by no means least of these personal tools at our disposal is our sense of smell. Experienced horse owners will frequently be able to spot when their horse is off colour by the smell of his coat and stable. A healthy horse has a fresh and clean smell regardless of whether he is covered in stable stains or just come in from a muddy field in a filthy condition. An unhealthy animal can have a quite distinctive 'off' and sickly odour that once encountered is easily recognized again. This sometimes rather unpleasant smell can be due to compounds excreted by the skin as the body tries to rid itself of toxins or other harmful matter. Be aware however that not all horses that are sick smell bad.

As with all mammals the horse's body is really a big tube with an entrance, the mouth, and an exit, the anus. Both inside and out the tube is covered and lined with a form of skin (epithelial tissue), some of it modified in one way or another to perform a variety of different functions. The mucous membranes of the lungs allow for the passage of oxygen into the blood stream and the lining of the gut facilitates the absorption of water and nutrient for maintenance of health and growth.

Solomon with Hilary taking five minutes out.

This book is designed to help the average horse owner in understanding the importance of keeping their horse's skin healthy and to give assistance and guidance in so doing. I hope it will equip the horse owner with a working knowledge of equine skin and its derivatives, how to maintain it in optimum condition and how to interpret the information it is giving us. Read and enjoy.

1.

Demystifying Descriptive Jargon

You will probably find some of this chapter quite hard going but please don't be put off as understanding the sections on the structure and function of skin and conditions and diseases will be made so much easier if you persevere. If you do decide to skip to the next chapter you can always refer back when you come across terms you don't understand.

There are some people who like to think they are in 'the know', who love jargon as a means of getting one over on the rest of us. However in most cases the primary function of this jargon is not to bemuse and befuddle but to provide a commonly understood, clear and concise means of describing exactly what is going on and to give a precise location on the body.

Not only do we need to be able to communicate signs and symptoms in detail but accuracy is also important when describing a horse for identification purposes, for example on a Thoroughbred passport and on the standard vaccination certificates. It is important that the terminology used for describing a horse is understood and in this chapter I have included detailed information on terms recommended for use for the purpose of identification, this nomenclature is doubly important now as all equines in the UK are required to have IDs of one kind or another.

Geographic Terms

When we want to find our way round in unfamiliar territory most of us use a map to get us from A to B, that is until we have got our bearings, and without doubt, the best way to describe and locate the points of the horse is by using a diagram, much like a map.

The points of a horse are used to pinpoint different areas of the body, all horse owners should be familiar with them and usually it is the first thing one learns when embarking on a relationship with horses even if you are only riding someone else's.

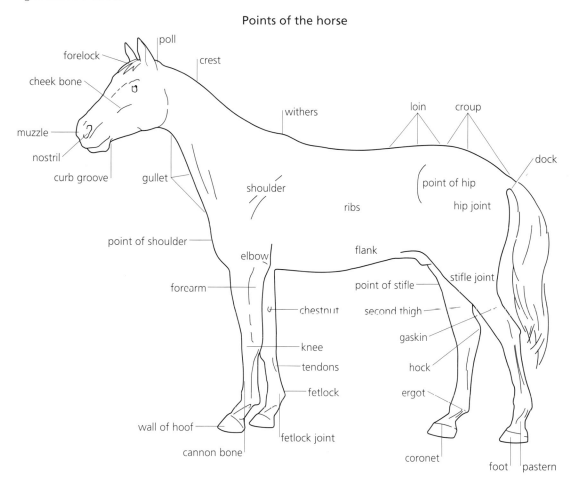

Points of the horse

Identification

Colour and markings are used to assist in the identification of a horse and as such it is important that they are accurately described and that we understand that description. In 1928 a subcommittee of the Royal College of Veterinary Surgeons was set up to investigate and recommend on a system of description of body colours, markings and other characteristics (which encompass blemishes) of horses and ponies to be used for identification purposes. The final report was published in 1930 since which time there have been a number of revised editions. It is interesting to note that the RCVS strongly recommend that the use of left and right as opposed to near and fore be adopted.

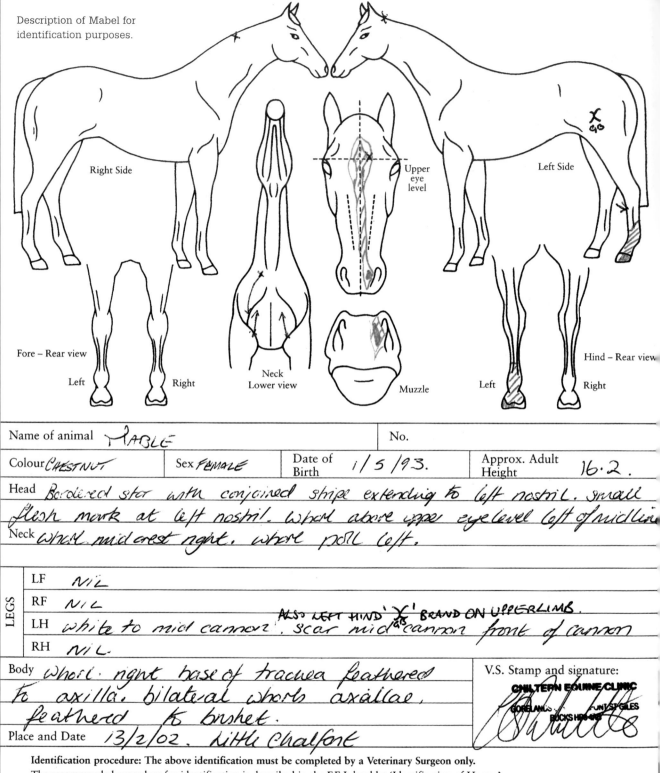

Description of Mabel for identification purposes.

Right Side

Left Side

Upper eye level

Fore – Rear view

Left   Right

Neck Lower view

Muzzle

Left   Right

Hind – Rear view

Name of animal	MABLE		No.	
Colour CHESTNUT	Sex FEMALE	Date of Birth 1/5/93.		Approx. Adult Height 16.2.

Head *Bordered star with conjoined stripe extending to left nostril. Small flesh mark at left nostril. Whorl above upper eye level left of midline*

Neck *Whorl mid crest right. Whorl poll left.*

	LF	*NIL*
LEGS	RF	*NIL*
	LH	*white to mid cannon. scar mid cannon front of cannon* ALSO LEFT HIND 'X' BRAND ON UPPERLIMB.
	RH	*NIL.*

Body *Whorl right base of trachea feathered to axilla. bilateral whorls axillae, feathered to brisket.*

Place and Date *13/2/02. Little Chalfont*

V.S. Stamp and signature:

CHILTERN EQUINE CLINIC
GORELANDS   FUN ST GILES
BUCKS HP8 4NS

Identification procedure: The above identification must be completed by a Veterinary Surgeon only.

The recommended procedure for identification is described in the F.E.I. booklet 'Identification of Horses'.

The diagram and written description must agree and must be sufficiently detailed to ensure the positive identification of the animal in future. White markings must be shown in red and the written description completed using **black ink in block capitals or typescript.** If there are no markings, this fact must be stated in the written description.

All head and neck whorls should be marked ("X") and described in detail. Other whorls should be similarly recorded in greys and in animals lacking sufficient other distinguishing marks. Acquired marks (" ") and other distinguishing marks, e.g. prophet's thumb mark ("Δ"), wall eye, etc., should always be noted.

Body Colours

These fall into two main categories, those colours accepted by Wetherbys for Thoroughbred horses, of which there are six, and any other colour.

Colours acceptable for Thoroughbred horses

- **Black** Black throughout the coat, mane and tail with no patterns other than white markings.

- **Brown** Black and brown in the coat with black limbs, mane and tail.

- **Bay** Variations in the body colour from light yellowish to dark reddish brown. Black mane and tail and distal parts of the limbs. Tips of the ears are also often black.

- **Bay brown** Body colour and muzzle brown with black limbs, mane and tail.

- **Chestnut** Colours range from yellowish to deep coppery bronze. Mane and tail the same colour as the body but may be a darker or lighter shade.

- **Grey** Body coat a mixture of black and white hairs on a black skin. A flea bitten grey may have a third colour in the coat.

A good example of a black horse although this one is not Thoroughbred but a Shire cross. Polo is an old horse so he now has quite a lot of white hairs in his coat. Many horses that are described as being black are not true blacks but extremely dark bay, true black horses being relatively uncommon.

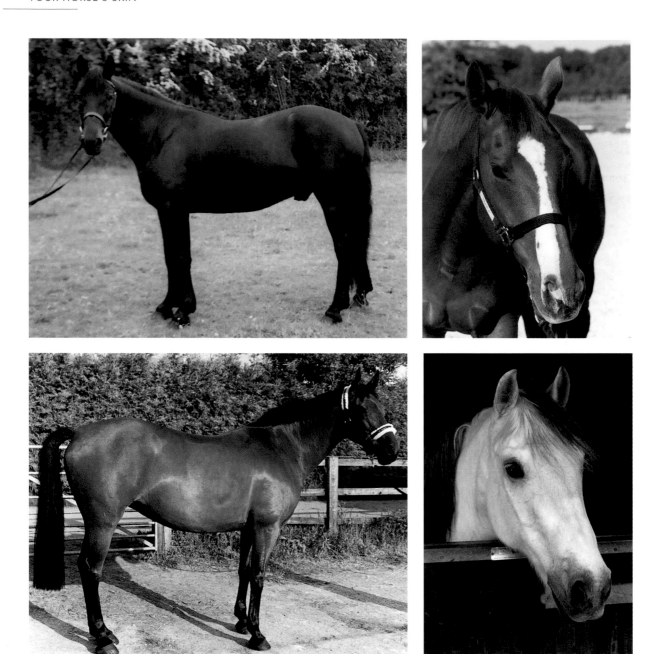

top left A very dark bay horse that when in full winter coat, could be mistaken for a black. Note the lighter colouring on the muzzle betraying the fact that this is not a true black.

top right Ryan, a chestnut horse with good rich colour to his coat.

bottom left Bee, a whole coloured, bay horse with no white markings. Characteristically this horse has a black mane and tail and black lower limbs. She also has black tips to her ears. The horse has very fine skin and coat as can be seen by the area resembling a rub behind the girth where the rider applies the leg aids.

bottom right Haley, a grey pony with an iron grey mane and tail. Grey horses get progressively lighter as they get older and can become almost white in colour. White horses are always referred to as greys unless they are albino or are completely pink skinned.

Other colours

Other colours are many and varied but some such as piebald and skewbald are not accepted by all breed societies. Of our native bony breeds only the Shetland allows piebald and skewbald coloured animals for entry in the stud book. In the main piebald and skewbald colouration is usually an indication of crossing and although this does not detract from the quality of the horse it does mean he has more than one breed in his ancestry.

- **Strawberry roan** Body colour a mixture of chestnut and white hairs. Mane, tail and limbs below the knees and hocks chestnut.

- **Blue roan** Body colour a mixture of black or black brown with white hairs. Black below the knees and hocks.

- **Bay roan** Body colour bay or bay brown with a mixture of white hairs. Usually black hairs below the knees and hocks.

- **Piebald** Large clearly defined patches of black and white.

- **Skewbald** Large clearly defined patches of any other definite colour and white.

- **Odd** Large irregular patches of more than two colours and white. Colours may merge and are not clearly defined.

- **Blue dun** Main, tail and skin black. Evenly distributed black in the body colour. May have a dorsal band or withers stripe.

- **Yellow dun** Black skin. Yellowish body hair. May have bars on the legs and a dorsal band or withers stripe. May have black on the limbs, head or tips of the ears.

- **Whole** No hairs of any other colour on the body.

- **Cream** Pink unpigmented skin. The iris may also be unpigmented giving the eye a pink or bluish appearance. Body colour is cream. Sometimes referred to as cremello.

- **Palomino** A shade of golden colour with a white mane and tail.

- **Appaloosian** Body colour grey with black or brown spots.

Markings

Because of the variation of shapes and sizes of various markings it is not possible to give an accurate written description without grouping them in some way. Even then the scope is too large for precision so all identification certifi-

Palominos frequently become darker with age, this horse, Jabina, is twenty-eight years old and still has a really good colour to her coat. The Palomino Society has quite strict rules about the depth of body colour, anything that is very light or very dark being unacceptable.

cates consist of a descriptive narrative and an outline drawing of the horse on which the markings are accurately indicated.

White marks

These are plainly visible against the main body colour of the horse, can be clearly defined or otherwise and be natural or acquired. Where the white marking contains varying amounts of hair of the general body colour it is said to be mixed. A marking that is outlined by a mixed edge is said to be bordered. An example of this would be a bordered blaze on the head. Coloured markings, for example black spots, on the white should be accurately described and marked on the diagram. As well as white markings a horse may have areas where the skin pigment is absent and these areas are known as flesh marks.

Head markings

- **Blaze** A broad white marking extending over and from the forehead down the face usually to the muzzle. The origin and termination of a blaze should be recorded along with any deviations and markings on the white.

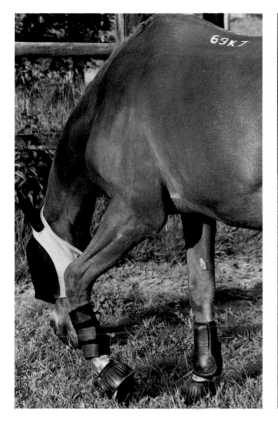

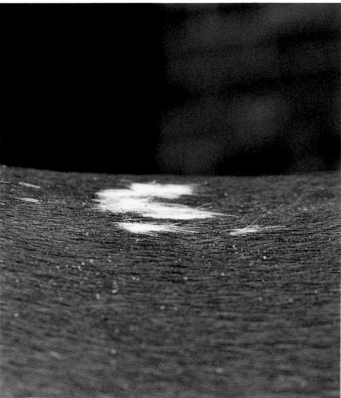

- **Stripe** A narrow white marking extending down the face. A stripe should not be greater than the width of the nasal bones. It is sometimes accompanied by a star to which it can be joined. It is then described as star and stripe conjoined. Any description of a stripe should include the points of origin and termination and any variations in direction or width. It should also include any marks on the white.

- **Star** A distinctive white mark on the forehead. A few white hairs in the center of the forehead should be described as such.

- **Snip** A white marking between or in the region of the nostrils that is independent of any other facial marking.

- **White face** A white marking covering the forehead, running down the front of the face to extend towards the corners of the mouth on either one or both sides.

- **White muzzle** White marking encompassing both lips and extending towards the nostrils.

- **Lip markings** Any marks on part or all of the lips should be accurately described and noted.

above left Acquired white marks, in this case freeze branding, deliberately inflicted as a means of identification.

above right Acquired white marks on the back of a horse from badly fitting tack, note the scurf in the coat.

above left Dermot, a nice honest face with a good example of a blaze.

above right Combined face markings. On Solomon's passport his head markings are described thus: 'Whorl midline above upper eye level. Star to left and above whorl conjoined to stripe and snip to both nostrils'.

right A flesh mark on Mabel's muzzle. Note the scar to the right of the flesh mark, both of these should appear on the passport as a means of identification. Flesh marks come in a variety of sizes and are characterized by an area of pink skin. Horses frequently have them on their muzzles where they are prone to sunburn so care should be taken to adequately protect these areas with a good sunblock.

Whorls

Whorls occur when there is a change in the direction of hair growth. They have been used for many years as a means of identifying a horse as they are more individual than other markings. Whorls come in various forms dependent on the junction of the directions of hair. Whorls are indicated by a cross on the diagram.

- **Simple** The hair appears to converge into a focal point. In a description this is simply noted as a whorl.

- **Sinuous** An irregular curved line where two opposing hair directions meet.

- **Feathered** A line along which two lines of hair meet. The hair growths, whilst in the same direction, are at an angle to one another giving the 'feather' appearance.

- **Crested** Line along which two opposite lines of hair meet from different directions. The hair rises up to form a crest.

- **Tufted** Simple whorl where the hair piles up to form a soft tuft.

- **Linear** The same as crested without the crest.

Other Identifying Marks

Body markings

- **Zebra marks** Stripes occurring on the legs, withers, neck or quarters.

- **List dorsal stripe** A line of black hair running from the withers down the centre of the back.

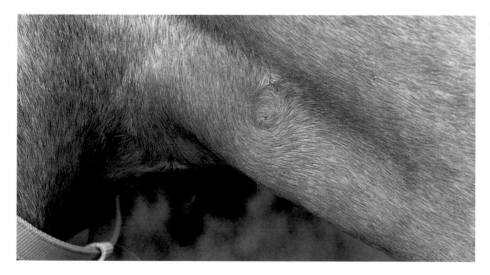

A nice clear whorl on Jebina's neck.

- **Patch** A clearly defined area of hair, different in colour from the main body hair.

- **Spots** Small roundish areas of differently coloured hair.

- **Black marks** Small areas of black hair anywhere on the body.

- **Grey-ticked** White hairs throughout the coat or on any part of the body.

- **Flecked** Little collections of white hairs dotted over any part of the body. A horse can be heavily or lightly flecked.

Mane and tail

For identification the position of any white or differently coloured hairs in the mane and tail should be noted.

Prophet's Thumb mark

Most often seen in Arab or Thoroughbred horses. A Prophet's Thumb mark has long been held as being a sign of a good horse. This is a depression in a muscle not unlike an indentation left by pressure of the thumb, hence the name. It usually occurs on the neck but can be found on the shoulder or rump. On an ID diagram it is indicated by a triangle and is noted in the written description. A Prophet's Thumb mark is a congenital abnormality.

Wall eyes

Another congenital abnormality where there is a lack of pigment in the iris giving rise to a pinkish or bluish-white appearance.

Flecking on the flank of a chestnut horse.

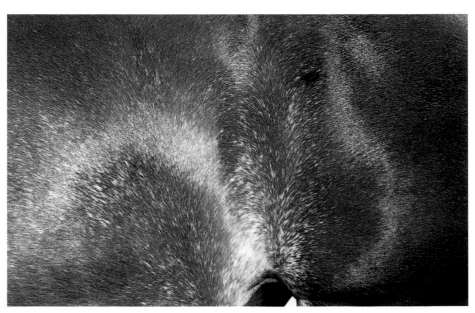

Showing the white of the eye

A horse is said to be showing the white of the eye when the white portion of the eyeball, or sclera, is visible around all or part of the dark bit of the eye. This is a congenital abnormality that can be present in one or both eyes. It is not necessarily a sign of a wild disposition.

Markings on limbs

The size and shape of white markings on the legs should be precisely described. The terms stocking and sock are no longer acceptable for the purposes of identification although they are still in common use when talking about horses. Instead a more accurate description of the extent of the marking should be given, for example 'white to mid cannon'.

Hoof marks

Variations in the colour of the hooves should be described. A horse with few identifying marks should have the characteristics and colour of the feet noted and in the case of greys the colour of each foot should be mentioned.

Acquired Markings

Acquired markings as opposed to congenital markings are permanent marks on the horse and include scars, tattoos, brands, harness marks, girth marks and firing marks. They are indicated by an arrow on the diagram and noted in the written description.

below left A brand of the British Hanoverian Society on the upper hind leg of a registered, pure bred mare.

below right A scar left by an old wound. Hair will not re-grow across this and the horse will now be described as blemished. This must have been quite a serious injury to have left this amount of skin damage. Incidentally the white mark on the leg is described as 'white to mid cannon'.

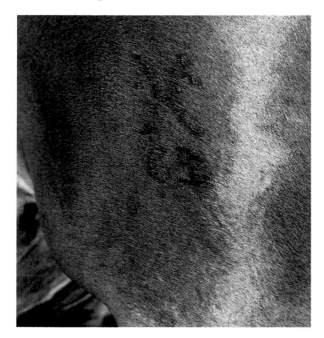

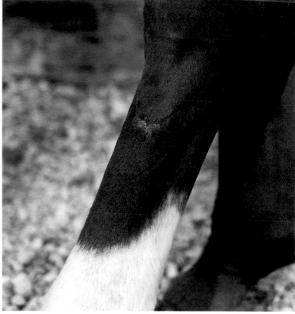

Anatomical Nomenclature

Being able to describe to your vet precisely what a skin condition looks like and where it is on the horse's body not only helps him in his clinical diagnosis but also has the effect of boosting your own confidence by making you feel less of an ignoramus.

The body is divided up by sections through it called planes within which, all movement can be described. These planes are:

- **Sagittal** The plane that divides the body into left and right halves.

- **Coronal** Divides the body into dorsal and ventral parts.

- **Dorsal** Relating to the back of the body or an organ.

- **Ventral** Relating to front of the body or an organ. In the case of the horse this refers to the belly.

When describing the location of a condition, terms are used which indicate its position relative to another area of the body. For instance the knee is superior (above) to the fetlock but inferior (below) to the shoulder.

Terms of location are:

- **Medial** Related to the central part of an organ, a tissue or the body.

- **Lateral** Anatomically the region or part of the organ or body that is furthest away from the medial.

- **Superior** Above in relation to an organ or part of the body.

- **Inferior** Below in relation to an organ or part of the body.

Clinical Terms

Jargon

Pathology tends to be described with either a suffix or prefix to an other descriptive word. For example bradykinesia meaning slow moving is made up of *brady* meaning slow and *kinesia* meaning movement. In the following list a dash (–) after the word denotes it is a prefix whilst a dash before a suffix.

A/An-   Low or absence of e.g. anaemia (aemia – of the blood)

Hyper-   Increased

Hypo-   Decreased

Eu-   Normal

Planes of the horse

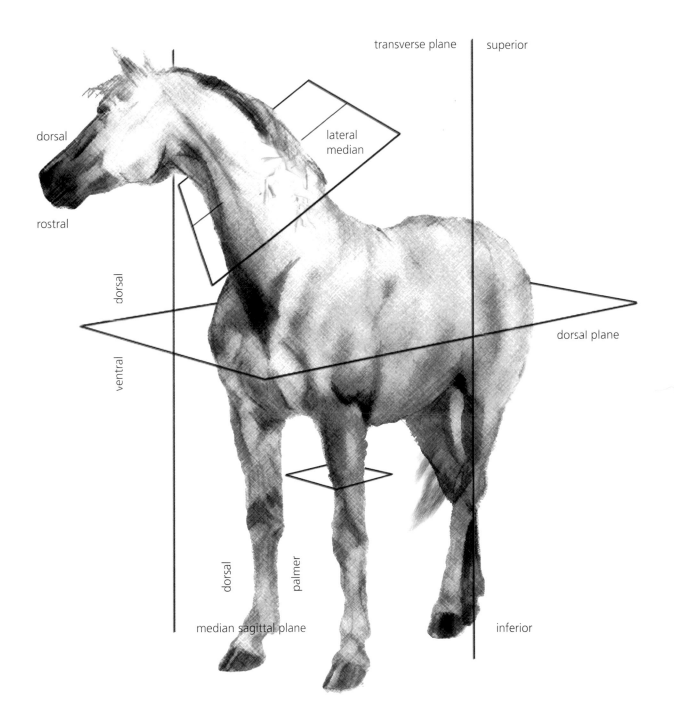

transverse plane

superior

dorsal

lateral
median

rostral

dorsal

ventral

dorsal plane

dorsal

palmer

median sagittal plane

inferior

Dys-	Difficult or away from normal
Tachy-	Fast
Brady-	Slow
-trophy	Growth e.g. atrophy – lack or absence of growth hypertrophy – increased growth
-plasia	Structure or form
Epi-	Covering/over e.g. epithelium
Peri-	Surrounding e.g. pericordial around the heart
Endo-	Inside/within
Cyst	Bladder or sac containing fluid

Pathological Terms

Rashes and Skin Conditions

Condition	*Description*
Abrasion	A minor wound affecting, in the context of this book, the surface of the skin or mucous membranes caused by erosion by scraping or rubbing. A graze is an abrasion.
Abscess	A localized collection of pus anywhere in the body caused by bacterial infection that the body's own defences have not been able to overcome. Abscesses are isolated from the surrounding area by inflamed and damaged tissue.
Bruise	A contusion. Rupture of underlying blood vessels causing discolouration of the skin from escaping blood. Bruising follows an injury.
Bullae	A blister more than 0.5 cm in diameter.
Contusion	A bruise of any kind.
Crust	Surface residue made up of dried serum, pus, blood and keratinous, bacterial and epidermal debris.
Dermatitis	Inflammation of the skin.

Condition	Description
Dermatosis	Any skin disease particularly one without inflammation.
Eczema	Specific inflammation of the skin.
Erosion	Wearing away of a surface by physical or chemical agents.
Erythema	Red rash of unspecified origin.
Eschar	A scab produced by the effect of heat or a corrosive substance on tissue.
Excoriation	The removal or destruction of the surface of the skin by any means. For example by scraping or the application of chemicals. Can also be caused by self mutilation.
Exfoliation	Removal of the outer layers of the skin. Also the sloughing off of dead skin cells.
Fissure	Anatomically this is a groove or cleft. Pathologically it is a crack in the skin or mucous membrane caused by disease.
Fistula	A passage between two hollow structures or a hollow structure and the exterior. Frequently caused by infection for example when an abscess bursts. Note: In horses, fistulous withers. This condition was generally brought about by badly fitting saddlery or harness, fortunately it is less common now than it has been in the past. Continuous trauma to the area from ill-fitting tack leads to the formation of an abscess with subsequent death of surrounding tissue (necrosis). As a result a sinus or fistula is formed which may be along any part of the wither. In unresolved cases the ligaments, spinous processes and cartilage in the region are commonly affected. Fistulous withers can also lead to secondary septicaemia.
Laceration	A tear in the skin and sometimes underlying tissue leaving a wound with irregular edges.
Lesion	Any abnormality of tissue structure or function that is caused by disease.
Macular	A flat rash.

Condition	Description
Macule	A circumscribed area of discolouration. This may be redder or paler than the surrounding skin and can be a different colour altogether.
Nodular	Hard red lumps that are often red and painful.
Nodule	A large papule. A small lump.
Papilloma	Lining tissue on a broad stalk.
Papule	A small raised area. A maculo-papular rash is both raised and discoloured.
Plaque	A large disc-shaped lesion.
Polyps	Lining tissue on a stalk.
Purpura	A skin rash resulting from bleeding into the skin from capillaries.
Pustules	Blisters filled with pus.
Rash	A temporary eruption on the skin, typically red in colour, either red spots or generalized reddening. Can be accompanied by itching. May be a local skin reaction or a sign of a disorder or infectious disease.
Scale	Accumulation of dead skin and other surface debris.
Scar	Tissue formed following an injury.
Ulcer	A break in the skin involving all the layers. Can be difficult to heal.
Vesicular	Blisters filled with a clear fluid.
Wheal	A discrete, well defined reddened swelling with a flat top and steep walled margins. It is produced by excessive fluid in the intercellular tissue spaces (oedema) in the dermis. This is usually associated with allergic reactions.

Descriptive Terms Used by Veterinary Dermatologists

Term	Description
Alopecia	Loss of hair where hair should be.
Asymmetrical	Uneven.

Term	Description
Term	*Description*
Depigmentation	Localized loss of normal colour from an area of skin.
Dermatology	A medical speciality to do with the diagnosis and treatment of skin disorders.
Dermis	The thick layer of living tissue under the epidermis of the skin. This is the true skin. It is made up of loose connective tissue containing blood capillaries, lymph vessels, sweat glands, sebaceous gland, hair follicles and nerve endings. Anything described as dermal relates to the skin.
Ectoparasite	A parasite that lives on the outer surface of the host. In horses lice are an example of an ectoparasite.
Epidermis	The outermost layer of the skin. It is divided into four layers.
Epithelium	This is the tissue that covers the external surfaces and lines the internal surfaces of the body. The epidermis is epithelial tissue.
Hyperpigmentation	More pigmentation than is normal.
Hypopigmentation	Less pigmentation than is normal.
Integument	The skin. From the Greek meaning whole body covering.
Keratin	A protein that is a major constituent of hooves, hair and the outermost layers of skin.
Keratinocytes	Type of cell found in and making up the bulk of the epidermis. Keratinocytes are produced in the deep layers and gradually migrate to the surface of the skin where they are sloughed off as dander. They contain a network of keratin filaments hence the name keratinocytes.
Langerhan cells	Cells in the skin that are important for generating the immune response.
Lichenification	Thickening of the epidermis which exaggerates the normal folds and creases of the skin. This is caused by excessive rubbing and scratching as can be seen in sweet itch.

Term	Description
Melanocytes	Skin cells that produce the skin pigment melanin.
Pruritus	Itching. This may be anything from mild to severe and is a symptom of a number of diseases.
Stratum basale	The deepest layer of the epidermis also known as the stratum germinativum. Rests on the basement membrane.
Stratum corneum	The top layer of the epidermis.
Stratum granulosum	The layer of the epidermis above the stratum spinosum but below the stratum corneum.
Stratum spinosum	The second layer of the epidermis above the stratum basale. Sometimes referred to as the prickle layer.
Subcutis	Tissue beneath the dermis. Not strictly part of the skin.

General

Term	Definition
Atrophy	Degeneration of cells leading to wasting of normally developed tissue.
Bacteria	A group of microorganisms that are considered to be more primitive than animals or plant cells because of their lack of a distinct nuclear membrane. They are widely distributed within the environment. Some bacteria produce disease which is caused by the release of toxins.
Configuration	Shape.
Exocrine	Exocrine glands release their secretions onto the surface by means of a duct.
Fauna	Animal life.
Flexion	Bending a joint so that the bones of that joint are brought towards each other. Extension is the opposite of flexion.
Flora	Plant life.
Fungi	Simple organisms that lack chlorophyll or green

Term	Description
	pigment. Some of them are parasites of animals and some cause disease (Singular is fungus).
Haematoma	An accumulation of blood within a tissue (skin) that clots to form a hard swelling. Caused by trauma, injury or disease.
Homeostasis	The mechanisms that the body employs in order to maintain a constant, stable, internal environment despite changes in the external conditions.
Hypertrichosis	Excessive growth of hair.
Hypotrichosis	Less than normal hair growth.
Induration	Abnormal hardening of tissue.
Inflammation	Tissue (the body's) response to injury. This can be acute or chronic.
Ischaemia	Reduction in the blood flow to an organ or tissue. If not corrected can lead to extensive tissue damage.
Necrosis	Death of some or all of the cells of a tissue or organ.
Oedema	Swelling which can be due to collection of fluid in the tissue. This is local when the swelling is due to injury or inflammation. Poor lymphatic drainage is a contributory factor.
Petechiae	Small, flat, round dark red spots caused by bleeding into the skin or under the mucous membranes.
Pityriasis	Dandruff. This is not in itself a disease but a clinical sign of a number of different diseases. Horses which are stabled with a low plane of nutrition and which are neglected and ungroomed often accumulate mild dandruff. It is important that the cause of pityriasis is ascertained.
Sinus	A blind cavity.
Tumour	A term usually applied to abnormal growth of tissue which can be malignant or benign.
Virus	A minute particle that is capable of replication but only if within another cell. They are instrumental in causing a number of diseases.

2.

The Function and Structure of Skin

We tend to think of the skin as a large sack enclosing and holding together all the other organs of the body but it is much more than an inert covering. The skin fulfils many complex functions and is a unique environment inhabited by a range of microscopic animals and plants known as the skin's flora and fauna. Moreover it is the only organ of the body that can be seen and is therefore the one most easily inspected and evaluated. As the largest organ of the horse's body in terms of surface area its efficiency is vital for continued health.

The skin is made up of epithelial tissue and is part of the body's immune system. Any surface in contact with the air and not sealed into the body cavity itself is covered with epithelial tissue of one kind or another. This includes the nasal passages and lining of the lungs and gut where the organ may be only one cell thick and is known as a mucous membrane.

As we have previously seen the condition of a horse's skin can tell you a lot about the general condition of the horse. Never mind the eyes being the windows to the soul, a horse's skin is the evidence of his health and fitness. As has been previously stated when we look at a horse what we see is the largest organ of the body. With practice we are able to evaluate the condition of this organ and make judgements as to general state of health. If we are observant the skin will inform all our senses of touch, sight and smell about the condition of the animal and give us insight into many sub-clinical conditions not yet manifest.

The skin, however, has other important functions apart from being a protective covering. Much of the time it is the part of the body most ignored and neglected, witness the quick flick round with a brush before we throw a saddle on to ride. We subject it to chaffing by ill-fitting tack and rugs and allow it to become waterlogged in muddy fields and yet despite our 'attentions' it is capable of repairing and regenerating itself thus continuing to carry out all its functions not least of which is the protection of the structures enclosed within.

The skin and associated structures, hair and hooves, plus muscles, nerves and various glands make up what is known as the integumentary system of the horse. The word integumentary is interpreted as 'inte' meaning whole and 'gument' meaning body covering. The purpose of the integumentary system is to protect and preserve the body's physical and biochemical integrity, to carry out functions to maintain a constant body temperature and provide the brain with information about the surrounding external environment

The Skin's Function

Whilst appearing to do nothing very much, except act as an inert sack to put the rest of the body in, the skin performs many important functions vital for the maintenance of the continued health of the horse.

As the largest organ of the body it protects the body against harmful radiation from the sun and all the other internal organs from physical and microbial trauma or damage. Numerous sensory nerves respond to variations in temperature and pressure by sending messages to the horse's brain about the external environment and when necessary warning of the danger of an imminent breach in these defences by causing a sensation of pain. In the normal course of events the skin also prevents the body from becoming dehydrated. It performs a regulatory function in terms of internal and external body temperature by the production of sweat to cool and by shivering to generate heat. The skin also acts as part of the endocrine system by producing the precursor for synthesising vitamin D, necessary for the up-take of calcium for strong bones, and it provides a route for the elimination of waste products. Variations in the thickness of skin exist over the horse's body the greatest thickness over the trunk and the thinnest on the face and abdomen. In addition to all this it is also capable, except in the most severe cases, of repairing itself when necessary. How important the skin is in carrying out all of these functions can clearly be seen by the life threatening situations that come about when even a relatively small area is damaged.

Protection

One of the primary functions of skin is as a dynamic physical, chemical and biological barrier between the external and internal environment. It protects against the sun's rays, absorbs trauma and prevents the entry of micro-organisms. It also guards against excessive moisture loss by retarding the evaporation of water from the body thus reducing the risk of dehydration and additionally, by the same process, slows down the entry of water to the body when, for instance, it rains.

However what we see when we look at a horse is a casing of lifeless hard and soft keratin. Beneath the layer of hair is the outer surface of the epidermis again composed of dead keratinous cells. Within this layer are exit channels through which sweat is excreted to cool the body and eliminate waste products. Hair follicles from which the hair grows each have a sebaceous gland that produce an oil called sebum. This lubricates the skin and keeps it supple and moist.

When sweat and sebum mix on the surface of the skin they produce bactericidal chemicals forming an acid mantle that kills surface bacteria and it is this that forms the first line of defence against infection.

Biological protection is provided by Langerhan cells within the epidermis that alert the immune system to the presence of potentially harmful invaders and by cells in the dermis called macrophages which consume bacteria and viruses that have managed to break through the surface.

By its presence the skin physically protects the internal body structures from damage and abrasion, rather like a glove which protects your hand from the outside environment.

Lastly and very importantly the skin guards against excessive water loss thus helping to prevent the horse from becoming dehydrated.

Sensation

The skin provides the brain with information about the external environment, notably pressure, temperature, touch and pain. This function is facilitated by receptors within the skin. Sensory nerves for monitoring minute changes in pressure and touch known as mechanoreceptors and nociceptors for the appreciation of pain, supply an ongoing stream of information through the peripheral nervous system to the central nervous system for the body to respond to. Interestingly touching an area can increase the blood supply to that area by 80 per cent.

Regulation

The skin contains sensory nerves for the detection of changes in external temperature called thermoreceptors. Most heat exchange takes place through the skin so not surprisingly it plays a major role in the control of body temperature and in the maintenance of homeostasis. The term homeostasis is used to describe the mechanisms by which a constant internal environment is achieved. Regulation of temperature in response to changes in the internal and external temperature of the body must all be catered for. The normal body temperature of an

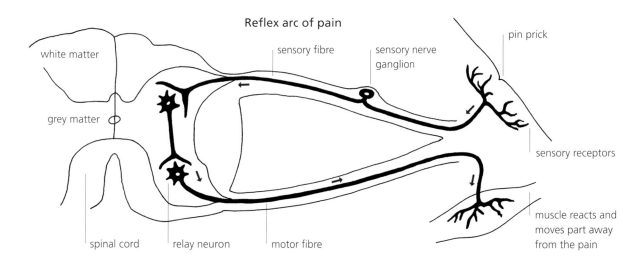

adult horse or pony of between 37° and 38° is affected by the degree of external temperatures, the presence of infection and by the level of exercise.

In addition to temperature regulation the skin plays an important part in regulating the electrolyte balance of the body. This is essential for the retention of water and important minerals.

Sweating

A horse will sweat when he feels hot in response to exercise or the ambient external temperatures as detected at the surface of the skin. Increase in certain hormones will also cause sweating when he is excited or afraid. In humans this latter type of sweating is called a cold sweat and has nothing to do with temperature regulation. Elevation of the body temperature results in stimulation of the sweat glands to produce sweat. Sweat is conveyed to the surface of the body where it evaporates. Heat loss results from the evaporation of water in the sweat causing the body to be cooled. In addition water diffuses upwards to the surface of the skin from the deeper layers and is continuously lost by evaporation even when sweat glands are not activated.

Heat loss from the skin is dependent on the amount of blood in the capillaries and vessels of the dermis. As the body becomes hotter the arterioles become dilated allowing more blood into the capillaries of the skin. This raises the temperature of the skin and thus increases the amount of heat lost by radiation, conduction and convection.

Shivering

Horses, like humans, shiver in response to feeling cold. Shivering is produced by a subcutaneous sheet of muscle, called the panniculous muscle, persistently contracting and thus moving the skin. In some instances this occurs locally to help dislodge flies and other parasites but overall shivering is used to generate heat and thus elevate the body temperature. Elevation of the body temperature is also assisted by the contractions of the arrector pilori muscles which raise the body hairs into a more upright position relative to the surface of the skin. This allows more air to be trapped next to skin reducing the heat loss by deepening the insulating layer. Although the arrector pilori is a very small muscle, contraction of a large number of these muscles can generate quite an appreciable amount of heat especially when in conjunction with contractions of the panniculous muscle resulting in shivering.

The Coat

In colder climates in winter the horse sheds his summer coat and grows a thick winter one to provide extra insulation and help keep him warm. The hair follicles from which the hair grows then enter a resting phase until the spring when the process is reversed. In the spring the follicles are stimulated into activity again and produce new hair that, by growing up through the follicles, dislodges the old coat that is then discarded.

Generally these actions of growing and shedding of hair are in response to shortening of length of day as winter approaches and the increase of daylight hours in spring and have nothing to do with the normal wear and tear of everyday life and the loss and re-growth of hair.

Hair is composed of dead keratinous cells forming an inert layer over the surface of the skin, however the hair itself is situated within a channel called a hair follicle which not only facilitates the secretion of sebum from the sebaceous gland onto the surface of the skin but also has a muscular attachment to raise the hair into a more vertical position. This muscle is called the arrector pilori muscle and it is made up of little bundles of involuntary muscle fibres attached to the hair follicles. It is stimulated by sympathetic nerve tissue responding to cold or fear.

When the body feels or detects external cold this muscle contracts raising the hair and trapping more warm air next to the surface of the skin. This helps to insulate the horse and prevent heat loss. Once the threat of cold has passed the muscle relaxes and the hair resumes its position flat against the skin. In addition the oily sebum coats the hair and skin surface giving additional insulation.

Because of this it is important we understand what we do when rugging up an unclipped, long-coated horse. The rug inevitably flattens the coat thus reducing the amount of warm air trapped next to the skin and preventing the horse's natural temperature regulatory system from working efficiently.

Arrector pili muscle – the process of raising and flattening the coat

Arrector pili muscles are found in all skin with hair where they have their origins and insertions in superficial dermis and the bulbous part of the hair follicle respectively. The largest arrector pili muscles are found along the dorsal part of the neck, the lumbar part of the back, the rump and the root of the tail. Occasionally when young horses challenge each other these hairs stand rather like the hackles of a dog.

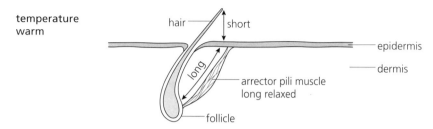

These muscles are important in thermo regulation. When a horse is cold the muscle contracts pulling the base of the hair follicle upwards towards the surface of the skin and raising the hair into a more upright position. This allows more warm air to be trapped against the skin surface thus keeping the horse warm.

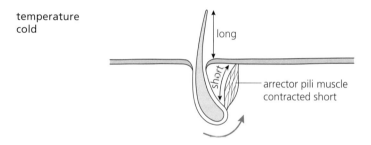

Once the body has warmed up the muscle relaxes and the hair sinks into a more horizontal position.

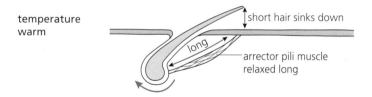

Excretion

As an excretory organ the skin plays a relatively minor role for the elimination of some substances including sodium chloride or salt, aromatic substances such as spices and urea, the latter particularly where there is impaired kidney function.

Part of the excretory function is facilitated by the sweat glands that are also involved in the regulatory role of the skin. Sweat contains a mixture of proteins (principally albumin), urea, uric acid, amino acids, ammonia and lactic acid and is excreted by glands lying in the skin. Salt is also excreted in sweat and excessive sweating can lead to low levels of blood sodium and dehydration unless intake of water and salt is appropriately increased. Minerals such as sodium directly impact on the electrolyte balance of the body. As we have seen previously sweating not only involves the elimination of waste products but also the control of body temperature.

To maintain good health it is essential that every horse has normal functioning sweat glands. The coils of the sweat gland, lying deep in the skin, are surrounded by a fine network of nerve fibres. These fibres terminate in the contractile tissue that releases sweat onto the surface of the skin. Each sweat gland is a tightly coiled tube lying deep in the dermal layer and is connected to the surface of the skin, by way of the hair follicle, by a tube known as a sweat duct.

Hairs also have a role to play in excretion principally of a number of minerals and it is known that the keratin of hair will take up arsenic. Other minerals excreted by hair are mercury, sulphur, zinc, copper, lead, selenium and iron.

Absorption

Until the late nineteenth century skin was thought to provide a totally impermeable and waterproof barrier for the body. Subsequent research found that it was permeable to some fat soluble substances (those that will dissolve in fat) whilst being relatively impermeable to water soluble substances (those that will dissolve in water). Those substances which are able to pass, go through the epidermis to the dermis and from there into the blood stream whilst others, because of their fat-loving nature, are stored in the subcutaneous layer beneath the dermis. It is well known that the lower skin layers act as a reservoir for topically applied substances that can then be released into the body should the fatty reserves be mobilized. This is not always desirable as the release of large quantities of stored agents into the bloodstream can, in extreme cases lead to toxic situations. It follows that we should always take care what and how much we apply to a horse's skin. In some cases the absorbed substances are altered by cutaneous enzymes, a process known as epidermal metabolism. These substances are then absorbed and are known as metabolites.

There are a number of factors that influence the rate of absorption into the skin. These factors can be categorized as biological, environmental, traumatic, vehicular and permeant.

Biological factors are affected by the thickness of the dead horny layer, the blood flow, the metabolic rate and the hydration of the skin. The thickness of the skin varies with the individual animal and with the location of the skin on the body. By and large the less hair covering there is the more a substance will gain access to the surface of the skin although the hair follicles and glands also provide a route for absorption. The blood supply to the skin is affected by, amongst other things, the external temperature and the greater the blood supply the more of the substance will be absorbed. Skin hydration changes with bathing, sweating, humidity, occlusion and application of products which form a film on the surface of the skin but it is water that affects the barrier performance of the skin more than any other non-irritant substance.

Environmental factors influencing absorption are the temperature, climate and time of day.

Traumatic factors are concerned with mechanical and chemical diseases, in fact anything which puts the skin under stress can be classed as traumatic.

Permeant factors are really concerned with the molecular weight and size of the substance being absorbed but in most instances this would be impossible for the horse owner to know. Some substances, for example essential oils, have such a small molecule that they easily pass through the skin and can be stored in the fatty subcutaneous layer beneath the dermis. These compounds are then retained by the body until the fat reserves are mobilized when they are released into the bloodstream. Whilst stored in the subcutis these compounds are relatively harmless but a sharp drop in body weight for whatever reason could result in a toxic level of the compound being made available to the rest of the body. From this you do not need to be Einstein to work out that we need to take care what we apply to the skin.

It is however important for the horse owner to understand how vehicular factors can affect absorption. These factors are the penetrating or permeant (see above) properties of the substance, the occlusion prevailing and the presence of a surfactant.

Occlusion occurs when the skin is covered by bandages, clothing, dressings, poultices, ointments or any other agent that prevents evaporation from the surface of the skin thus increasing the hydration and raising the temperature. To put this in context imagine bringing your horse in from a muddy field and immediately bandaging his legs without cleaning and drying them first. Warm moist conditions that increase the permeability of the skin added to a sealed in 'dressing' of infective agents and you can imagine the consequences that might ensue.

Surfactants such as detergents and soaps found in shampoos and body washes also affect the absorption of the skin. These seem to affect the skin's water binding capacity and it has been shown that when used alongside some anti-microbial agents can positively affect the absorption of the agent into the skin.

Secretion

The secretion function of the skin is carried out by the sebaceous glands. These open into the hair follicles and are present in all parts of the body where there is hair. They release an oily substance, known as sebum, which keeps the hair soft and pliable and provides the gloss on the coat. On the surface of the skin sebum penetrates the top layer to prevent cracking and drying and to provide some waterproofing. When mixed with sweat it also acts as an antibacterial and anti fungal agent helping to prevent invasion of the body by microbes.

Endocrine Function

The skin also acts as an endocrine organ for synthesizing vitamin D, necessary for the uptake of calcium. This function is carried out by a precursor molecule present in the skin that is activated only in the presence of sunlight. Vitamin D deficiency leads to a condition known as rickets both in humans and in horses but as D is a fat soluble vitamin which can be stored in the body care should be taken when feeding supplements.

Immunity

Broadly speaking immunity is the way the body recognizes, disposes of and defends against anything which is non-self. Within the immune system there are considered to be two pathways specific and non-specific. The skin and mucus membranes, both of which have mechanical and chemical barriers, are a first line of defence in the non-specific path.

Skin

Because of its tough and waterproof (cronified) layers skin is very resistant. However if the integrity of the skin is compromised by cuts, abrasions, burns or surgical incision etc, invasion by micro-organisms can easily and frequently does take place. In circumstances where the skin remains moist or becomes water-logged, infection is common, as in the case of mud fever in wet winter conditions.

The fatty acids, the chemical components of fat, found on the surface of the skin are known to kill bacteria and the salt in sweat inhibits the growth of many of them.

The lining of the gut

Helpful bacteria existing in a symbiotic relationship with the horse as host, populate parts of the skin lining the gut. These bacteria, known as the flora of the gut, create an environment that disadvantages the growth of other more harmful bacteria. Antibiotics are known to disrupt this balance by indiscriminately killing off the good bacteria and allowing the harmful bacteria to proliferate.

Mucous membranes

Mucous membranes do not have the keratinized layer that skin has and the epithelial layer secretes mucus that lubricates and moistens the surface. Mucus is slightly viscous and traps bacteria and other foreign bodies such as dust particles. The mucous membrane of the nose has hairs that filter and clean the air, trapping microbes and dust.

Communication

Horses in their natural environment are creatures that thrive on physical contact, standing close to one another and indulging in mutual grooming. This activity is known to reduce heart rate and lower blood pressure. Many horses are deprived of this mode of communication with their peers, being kept in stables and individual paddocks on a 'you can look but not touch' basis. This is unfortunate as a horse will determine his status within a group by this kind of communication through the skin. We have all watched them with pleasure and apprehension squealing and stamping feet after touching muzzles but who amongst us has witnessed this when no touching has taken place? We also have a penchant for snipping off those long cat hairs on the muzzle thus reducing the communication a horse has with his immediate environment.

The skin on the muzzle is very fine and sensitive as indeed are the lips. One of my own horses can sort out a powder wormer from his feed and leave it in a neat little pile at the side of his bowl no matter how well it is mixed in to a dampened feed.

Reservoir for Blood

The dermal layers of skin are richly supplied with blood. The blood vessels dilating and contracting determine the amount of blood close to the surface of the skin. Large quantities of blood close to the surface help the body temperature keep in balance. When a horse is startled this reservoir comes into use to supply the main muscle groups used for flight, the capillaries in the skin contract thus reducing the blood supply that is then diverted elsewhere in the body. If at this point we could see the horse's skin beneath the coat it would be paler in colour.

The Structure of the Skin

The skin of the horse has physically three layers, the dermis, epidermis and finally a layer of hair, the latter of which is an epidermal derivative assisting in the regulation of body temperature and excretion of some minerals. There is also a deeper layer called the subcutis beneath the dermis but this is not strictly speaking part of the skin although I have included information about it.

The skin itself is formed by a number of different tissue types and can be

Anatomy of the skin

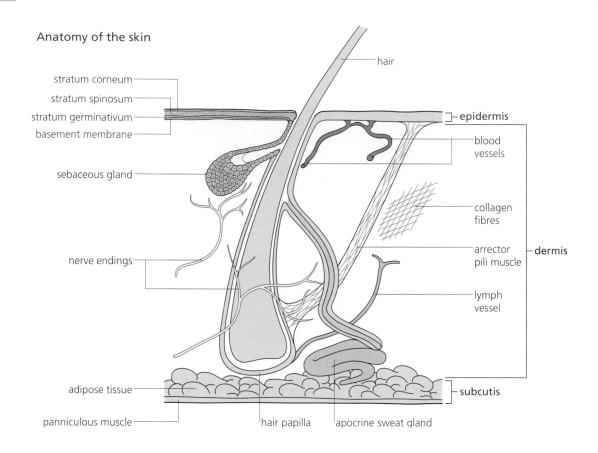

divided principally into two parts, the epidermis and the dermis with the sub-cutis lying below the dermis. The thickness of the skin varies over different parts of the body the thinnest being on the face, lower neck and abdomen with the thickest along the back. The mucous membranes are finer still and are in some places only one cell thick.

Epidermis

The epidermis rests upon a basement membrane and contains four principal types of cells. These cells types are keratinocytes, the main cells that produce keratin, melanocytes, producing melanin (pigment for the determination of colour), Langerhans cells which are part of the immune system and are very sensitive to ultra violet light and merkell cells conveying the sense of touch.

The main function of Langerhans cells is to direct antigens, substances that stimulate the production of antibodies, to lymphocytes for further processing.

The first layer, the stratum basale or stratum germinativum, is formed of a single row of columnar cells capable of continuous cell division resting on a basement membrane. These cells produce a family of identical daughter cells called keratinocytes that migrate slowly to the surface. During this process they

Epidermis

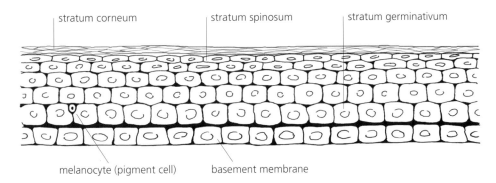

mature, lose their nucleus, keratinise and die before being sloughed off. On this journey to the surface they also acquire pigment and having reached a transitional area die and become part of the stratum corneum.

Maturation and keratinization takes place in the layer above the stratum basale known as the prickle layer or stratum spinosum.

In the next layer, the granular layer or stratum granulosum, the cells begin to show different stages of degeneration with the presence of the precursor of keratin. The final layer, the horny layer or stratum corneum is a layer of flat dead cells filled with keratin, these cells provide a strong barrier against heat, light, bacteria and chemical and mechanical substances and are eventually sloughed off as dander or scale as the next layer moves up to replace them. The epidermis itself has no blood supply and receives all its nutrition from the deeper layers of skin.

The area where the epidermis and the dermis meet is defined by the basement membrane and is known as the basement membrane zone or dermal-epidermal junction. This has important stabilizing, filtering and barrier properties. The renewal time of epidermal cells is around seventeen days, growth of epidermal cells is stimulated by a hormone known as the epidermal growth factor or EGF.

Epidermal Derivatives

Epidermal derivatives are structures that originated from epidermal tissue but have become specialized. Hair, the outermost layer, is lifeless and formed of hard keratin – a substance composed of pure protein. It is an epidermal derivative and is made up of a string of keratinized cells stuck together. The hair follicles are formed as a joint effort between the dermis and the epidermis in utero by down-growths of the epidermis. Following birth no more hair follicles are formed so if, for any reason, they die no more hairs will be produced by those follicles and the area involved will remain bald.

As we have seen previously, the epidermis has no blood supply of its own. In order to supply the hair follicle with blood and nutrition a specialized structure from the dermis called the dermal papilla becomes intimately associated with the hair.

The root of the hair lies deep in the dermis, occasionally even deeper in the subcutaneous layer. Attached to the root of the hair are oil glands and smooth muscle cells with nerve root endings, which are sensitive to touch around the hair follicle.

As preparation for winter months in cold and temperate climates, added insulation in the form of long hair is produced. The hair follicle then passes into a dormant state until springtime when the length of day increases stimulating the follicle into activity again. Old hair is dislodged by new hair growing up through the follicles and in this way the coat is renewed annually. The exception to this is the mane and tail where the hair may continue to grow for several years. A horse has two main types of hair, the vellus hairs, which are soft and downy and the long more bristly guard hairs. The hairs surrounding the muzzle are vibrissae hairs or whiskers. These are specialized sensory hairs with an extensive and complicated blood and nerve supply.

The sebaceous or oil glands produce sebum, a mixture of fats, cholesterol, protein and inorganic salts. The secreting part of the gland lies in the dermis and opens into the hair follicle. The oil produced by these glands is especially important to horses and ponies living out as it plays a vital role in keeping the horse warm in cold conditions.

Sweat glands are also formed from the down-growths of the epidermis. They are less well developed on the middle of the back and limbs than on the rest of the body. Horse sweat is a protein-based substance with the main protein being albumin. The sweat glands in a horse open out via a duct into the hair follicle and are not the same as those in people. They are triggered both by sympathetic and parasympathetic stimulation resulting in a totally different way of sweating from humans.

Both the sympathetic and the parasympathetic nervous systems are divisions of the autonomic nervous system (ANS) which together with the endocrine system, regulate the organs of the body. The activity of the ANS is regulated by the hypothalamus, an area of the brain. In effect the sympathetic and parasympathetic nervous systems are in opposition so whilst one excites the body the other calms or inhibits. It is this complementary action that maintains homeostatis.

The sympathetic nervous system is involved in preparing the body to respond to emergency situations, the fight or flight response. This comes into play when a horse experiences fear or anxiety or in fact any emotional disturbance, real or imaginary. During what the horse perceives to be an emergency situation the sympathetic nervous system reacts quickly to divert resources away from areas such as the skin and digestion to others that can increase muscular power should rapid flight be necessary. The object of the exercise is to increase blood flow, and thereby oxygen to the muscles. To do this, the heart rate increases, the peripheral blood vessels constrict, the bronchioles dilate and there is an increase in blood pressure.

Conversely the parasympathetic nervous response represents the body at rest. This returns the body's resources to all the organs so that normal function can be restored. The heart and respiratory rate returns to normal as does the blood pressure, the gastric functions and elimination processes resume and there is vasodilatation thus returning the blood supply to the skin and other organs.

Constant stress means that the sympathetic nervous response is constantly active depriving the body of rest and thereby normal function.

Hooves are a type of skin as are the eyes, with the exception of the retina, even a mare's udder is formed of specially modified sweat glands.

Dermis

The dermis is a much thicker layer than the epidermis and is composed of connective tissue, including an interwoven mass of collagen and elastic fibres with comparatively few cells in a gel-like ground substance. This enables the dermis to be both flexible and supportive as a substrate for the epidermis. It is in this layer of the skin that blood and lymph vessels, sensory corpuscles and autonomic and sensory nerves are found. The cell components of the dermis are fibroblasts and mast cells.

Functionally the dermis takes part in the immune response, provides a barrier against internal or external infection, synthesizes collagen for elasticity, responds to hormones and contains enzymes.

Blood Supply

To fulfill its many functions the skin requires a significant blood supply. This is provided by a rich vascular system lying within the dermis. Arterioles, deep in the dermis, deliver nutrients and systemically administered medicines or drugs to the skin whilst carrying absorbed products to the rest of the body.

The vascular system is also important in the skin's reaction to infectious agents, response to trauma, promotion of healing, control of body temperature and the degree of colour of the skin.

Subcutis

Strictly speaking the subcutis is not part of the skin but is the layer beneath the dermis consisting of fatty connective tissue to which, for mobility, the skin is loosely attached. A sheet of muscle called the panniculus muscle is able to move the skin by persistent contraction in order to generate heat where necessary (shivering) and to dislodge parasites. The subcutaneous layer serves as a storage depot for fat and contains the large blood vessels that supply the dermis. It also acts as a cushion against the rough and tumble of everyday life.

Thickness of the Skin

The thickness of a horse's skin varies over the surface of the body being thinnest on the face and lower limbs and thickest over the back. As far as other domestic animals go the horse is thicker skinned than either sheep or pigs but thinner skinned than cattle.

Skin and Coat Colour

There is an old saying that a good horse is never a bad colour and daft as it may seem there is a grain of truth in this. One of the first things a vet will look at when examining a horse is the colour of the membranes around the eyes, inside the nostrils and the gums. This can tell him a great deal about the condition of the horse and can assist in diagnosis. For example liver disease often manifests itself by yellow colouration of the membranes caused by the presence of bilirubin, a by-product of the breakdown of bile, in the blood.

Due to the covering of hair over the body the membranes inside the nostrils, around the eyes and the gums are the easiest areas of skin to examine for indications that all is not as it should be. There are a number of factors that affect the colour of skin and mucous membranes. These are the amount of blood in the skin, the amount of oxygen in the blood, the amount of bile pigments and carotenes in the blood, the amount of melanin the skin contains and genetic factors.

Of the above list only the first four are concerned with the health of the horse whilst the last is how the colour of the coat and normal colour of the skin is determined.

Warm conditions or exercise will predispose an increase in the blood supply to the skin in order to maintain or reduce the body temperature. This increase can be seen as a degree of redness, the greater the blood supply the redder the skin will become. This is also the case with the presence of infection where the blood supply is increased to fight the inflammation. Similarly a horse with depleted oxygen supply in the blood will show pale skin and membranes with possibly a bluish tinge.

In order to understand what is happening to produce these colour changes we have to know more about the body chemistry of the horse, a subject which

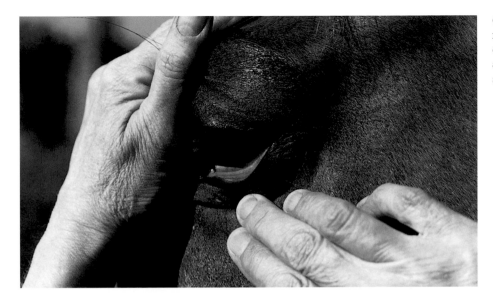

Good healthy mucous membranes around the eye. These membranes are a good medium salmon pink colour.

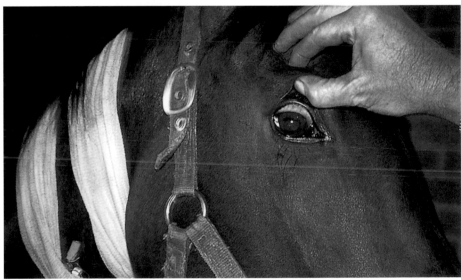

In this case the mucous membranes are very yellow and the horse is jaundiced.

is not covered in this book, however it is worth mentioning that there are a number of specific diseases that will significantly affect the colour of the skin. More information can be found on these in the chapter on conditions and diseases.

Genetic factors dictate the colour of the coat and basic skin colour. In genetics the number and type of genes a horse is carrying is known as its genotype whilst the phenotype is what it looks like outwardly. The phenotype of a horse or pony can be seen but the genotype unfortunately cannot. A horse's characteristics are inherited from its sire and dam via genes that are arranged in specific patterns along a pair of chromosomes found in the nucleus of every cell. Of the chromosomes, which are always in pairs, one is inherited from the sire and one from the dam. The position of a gene on a chromosome is called the gene locus and as chromosomes come in pairs each individual can have two copies of each gene.

Simply, if an animal has two genes (one from each parent) that are the same it is said to be homozygous for that gene, if they are different it is heterozygous. Now, a gene can be dominant or recessive or it can be additive in conjunction with its mate. This means that in a heterozygous partnership the dominant gene will always be expressed whilst a recessive gene will always be suppressed. For example if a bay horse which is homozygous, i.e. both genes for colour are bay, is mated to a chestnut horse which is also homozygous the resulting foal will be a heterozygous bay as bay is a dominant gene the chestnut gene having been suppressed. However a bay horse that is heterozygous carrying a recessive chestnut gene, mated to a chestnut horse, may produce a heterozygous bay or a homozygous chestnut.

There is a congenital condition called Lethal Dominant White that involves a dominant gene producing a white foal with blue eyes. If this gene is inherited from both parents i.e. the offspring is homozygous, the foal dies in utero and it follows that all white horses possessing a dominant white gene are therefore heterozygous. The reason the foal dies in utero is not known.

Many breed societies will only allow a certain range of colours outside of which the animal will not be accepted for registration in the studbook as a pure bred example of the breed. Native pony breed societies for example, with the exception of the Shetland, do not accept piebald or skewbald entrants.

Many years ago horses of certain colours were frowned upon in the show ring and even an exceptional skewbald would have been placed last in a group of indifferent bays and chestnuts. Thankfully this is now a thing of the past. I dislike wishy washy colour of any hue particularly chestnut which brings us back to the saying 'a good horse never being a bad colour'.

3.

The Skin in Sickness and in Health

I t is no accident that when we want to convey how well something looks we describe it as being a 'picture of health'. When we see a horse bursting with health and vitality we instinctively know it is 'right' without actually knowing how we know this. This is where we demystify that process.

More than half the sensory receptors of the human body are located in the eyes and a large proportion of the cerebral cortex of the brain is given over to processing the visual information that the eyes receive. The interpretation of what we see, once we have a benchmark to make judgments against, happens very rapidly when we have learnt to believe in and trust ourselves. It is this ability we want to harness to enable us to spot signs of illness at a very early stage.

However vision is not the only sense that can be employed when assessing the relative health of a horse's skin. Touch is equally important as the feel of a horse's coat can convey a great deal with regard to general health status. In addition as well as the visual and tactile senses the sense of smell also provides important information, if to a lesser degree.

Indications of Healthy Skin

First things first. Let us consolidate our existing skills and understand what we are looking for in terms of the signs of health. Visually a healthy horse will have an alert expression and will stand four-square evenly on each leg, however in this book, we are interested primarily in the skin and what we can glean from our observations of its condition.

Mabel, glowing from the inside out. No artificial sprays or products have been applied to her coat so the bloom is from robust good health. Mabel lives out in the summer and gets plenty of good natural herbage, good quality energy feeds when she is working hard and plenty of fresh air and exercise.

The Coat

The coat should be glossy and lie flat against the skin with no uneven patches. The hair of the coat varies greatly between the different types of horse, coarse on a native pony to the fine hair of a Thoroughbred, but whatever the breed or type the hair should not look or feel dull and lifeless or sticky. In addition one of the most obvious signs of good general health is a good coat with a good clean smell.

In a healthy animal the distribution of the hair should be even with no bald patches although there are obviously parts of the horse's body that have less hair than others, for example on the inside of the hind legs above the hocks. Also it is a good idea to get to know the colour of your horse's coat when he is in full health as this can sometimes vary when a horse is not so well and is in other words 'off colour'. Personally I find this most noticeable with chestnut horses as, in my experience, the coat becomes pale and dusty looking.

The Skin

Healthy skin should be supple and mobile over the underlying structures. It should not feel hot to the touch and should spring back into shape when it is pinched, this is called the tenting test. There should be no signs of sweating, which cannot be explained away by exercise, and no sign of weeping. The integrity of the skin should be intact and not compromised by injuries or sores with the surface free from scurf and parasites. Look for any raised areas of hair or growths such as warts and sarcoids.

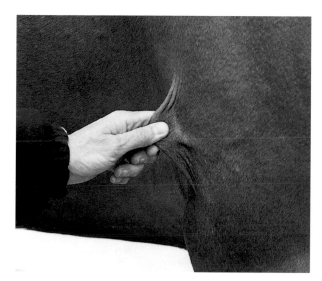

above Pinching the skin out in the tenting test. This is an excellent way of assessing the condition of the skin and is particularly useful for gauging the level of dehydration. The skin is pulled out as shown in the photograph and released. Provided the skin is not tight through illness or the horse is not dehydrated it will spring back into place within three seconds. Solomon's skin has sprung back within the three seconds (*above right*) demonstrating that his skin is in good condition and that he is not suffering from dehydration.

right An area of rough hair such as this gives an indication that the skin is not totally healthy. This pony has been rubbing in response to some kind of irritation. The cause should be investigated.

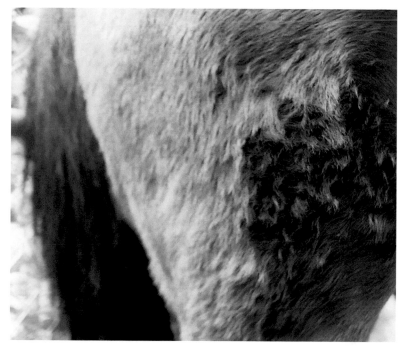

The Mucous Membranes

The thing to remember about mucous membranes is the colour they should be in a healthy animal. Generally they should be a medium salmon pinkish colour and nicely moist not dry. The most usual place to inspect the mucous membranes is around the eye by slightly pulling down the lower lid to expose a section of sclera or by inspecting the gums. However, remember that some horses have darkly pigmented gums which is quite normal and not an indication of disease.

Mucous membranes, particularly the gums, that are too pale may indicate anaemia, a high worm burden or chronic indigestion but they can also become suffused with blood presenting a dark purplish-blue appearance sometimes indicative of shock. In the case of serious illness the mucous membranes can take on a very obviously different colour as in the case of liver disease leading to jaundice. In this case the mucous membranes become yellow in colour. In pneumonia the membranes become red with a blue tinge, deep red membranes are indicative of fever and blue red membranes may lead us to suspect heart disease or circulatory problems.

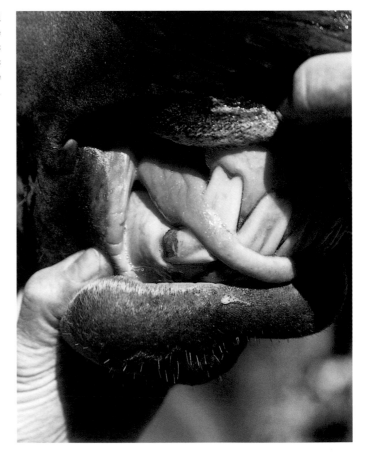

A horse in good health. Note the colour of the gums and mucous membranes on the inside of the mouth.

Apart from the colour, the gums are a useful place to test for circulatory problems. This is a simple test called a press test and is very easy to perform. Retract the lip and press a finger firmly on the gum, which will turn white, release the pressure and the gum should return to the normal colour within three seconds. Any longer may indicate a problem with the horse's circulation. In veterinary terms this is known as the capillary refill time.

Signs of Illness

Now you know what the signs of health are it will be much easier to recognize signs of illness either in terms of actual skin diseases or other diseases that are reflected in the skin. Predictably the signs of disease are the opposite of the signs of health. The skin may be tight with little or no mobility. When pinched it may not immediately return to normal but stay peaked, this usually indicates a level of dehydration. The skin may be dirty and covered in scurf or infested with parasites. You may not be able to see these but you will certainly be able to identify their droppings. Horses that are sick frequently have a harsh, staring coat, by that I mean that the hair stands up from the skin and is coarse and

Scurf and grease in the tail. A good grooming regime will prevent the build up of dead skin and dirt. Skin parasites would be more than happy with this sort of environment but a good grooming regime will help prevent a build up like this of dead skin and dirt.

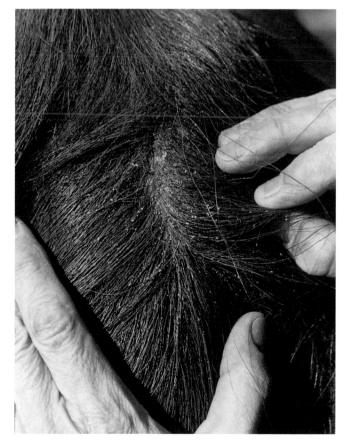

dry to touch. There may be areas of heat or cold and there may also be swelling. Look for sweating not related to exercise and note any unpleasant smells.

Other signs of ill health to look for particularly in the coat and skin are, alopecia and retention of the coat. The latter is commonly referred to as hirsutism but this is an incorrect term as it actually pertains to women who have unusual patterns of hair growth. Coat abnormality in horses, as seen with Cushing's disease, is properly called hypertrichosis. This specifically refers to hair length and density outside of the norm for age and type.

A number of different conditions will cause alopecia which can also be due to self inflicted trauma by biting or rubbing and many skin ailments are characterized by pruritis, a symptom of disease and not a disease in itself. A horse that rubs or bites himself does so to scratch an itch that may be so intense he damages himself in an effort to relieve it. Itchy skin disorders include sweet itch, insect bites, urticaria, contact and allergic dermatitis, parasites, photosensitivity and pemphigus foliaceous.

Mechanical injuries such as cuts and abrasions, whilst not signs of disease in themselves, can very rapidly lead to disease conditions if they are neglected and allowed to fester and any degree of pain or sign of pus should be investigated immediately.

The Skin Under Stress

There are four possible groups of factors that cause the malfunction of the skin. These are:

- External factors causing mechanical damage to the skin such as cuts, abrasions and burns. These external factors would also include damage caused by rugs and badly fitting tack for example saddle sores.

- External factors but due to the body's inability to deal with the causative agent. For example chemicals causing contact dermatitis and bacterial, fungal or viral infections as in the case of mud fever.

- Internal factors indicating problems within the body like eczema, high worm burdens, Cushing's disease, liver disease and immune mediated diseases like Coronary Band Dystrophy.

- Internal factors caused by poor nutrition, plant poisoning or dehydration.

Factors Affecting Health

There is very little to go wrong with a horse that is well nourished, has good housing, plenty of exercise and fresh air, companionship of his own kind, and an owner who is sensitive to his needs. Anything outside of these parameters over the long term will put a strain on the system and things will start to go wrong. In many cases it may not have a direct impact on the skin but eventually it will be reflected in the skin's condition.

Excess of heat or cold leads to sweating or shivering both of which require energy expenditure and therefore more calorific intake. A horse that sweats under the burden of an over warm rug will require extra food in the same way as one that is without a rug in very cold weather. Being overheated is probably more distressing for the horse as they appear to be able to handle being on the chilly side better than being too hot.

Lack of food over a period of time will have very serious consequences as all the body systems require food to produce energy and for growth and repair. This is very true of the skin which heals much more slowly in poorly nourished or dehydrated animals.

Bullying in the field can also have a detrimental effect on your horse's health and in this case can affect the skin in particular. If your horse comes in from grazing with bite and kick marks or is not doing as well as he perhaps should, check if he is being bullied by one or more of the other horses in the field and either remove the bully or your horse. Another situation that predisposes ill health is stress resulting from cruelty, overwork, constant fear, loneliness and ongoing pain from badly fitting tack.

In an ideal world it would be possible to avoid all hazardous and potentially challenging situations but horse owners frequently have to compromise, indeed many of them are not aware they are doing so which is why so many thing go wrong so frequently.

Inflammation

The inflammatory response is one of the most important aspects of skin disease and can be defined as the reaction of a tissue, such as skin, to trauma of any kind. Apart from the staring coat found with general debility and a number of other internal conditions one of the first signs of skin disease is inflammation. Inflammation is a physiological response to injury to tissue that is characterized by a series of events local to the damage. It has a number of different functions, the purpose of which are to protect the body by isolating, inactivating and removing the cause of the problem and any damaged tissue so that healing can take place.

As part of the body's non-specific defence mechanism, inflammation can be caused by a number of different factors, but in each case the body's inflammatory response is the same. Common causes of inflammation are bacteria or microbes (infection), physical factors such as cuts, heat, cold, radiation and mechanical injury, foreign bodies such as splinters, organic chemicals such as weed killers, toxins produced by microbes, inorganic chemical such as acids and alkalis and irritants which stimulate the immune system into action as in an allergic response. Basically there are two types of inflammation, acute and chronic.

Acute Inflammation

This is usually rapid in onset, short lived and can range from mild to severe. As with chronic inflammation where the response is less marked it is characterized by a number of signs.

- Redness

- Heat

- Pain

- Swelling

- Reduction in function

These signs indicate specific changes in the tissue and are a warning that all is not well. However it is as well to note that inflammation and infection are not the same thing although infection will cause inflammation.

Chronic Inflammation

With chronic inflammation the processes are much the same but with the following differences. It is generally less severe than the acute form and occurs over a much longer period of time with a much slower onset. It may follow on as a complication from a bout of acute inflammation that has not been completely resolved or a primary condition that is slow to develop. It may also develop insidiously as a result of persistent irritation, infection by a specific type of bacteria or an abnormal immune response covering a long period of time. In contrast to acute inflammation there is much more destruction of tissue with more fibrosis and all the attendant far reaching consequences. Frequently chronic inflammation goes unnoticed for extended periods of time.

The Inflammatory Response

The whole process starts with an injury of some kind compromising the integrity of the tissue, which in our case, is the skin. This bodily response isolates the injury and prepares the site for healing. Blood vessels in the area dilate (vasodilation) allowing more blood carrying oxygen and nutrients to the area and causing the characteristic redness and heat. Cells damaged by the injury release substances called chemical mediators, the complex actions of which I shall not attempt to describe here. The walls of the tiny blood vessels (capillaries) carrying blood to the site, become more permeable allowing protein and water to leave the bloodstream as a clear fluid called exudate and this collects in the interstitial spaces causing swelling. Swelling in turn compresses the sensory nerve ending resulting in tenderness and pain. Triggered by the inflammation white blood cells (leucocytes) move to the site of the injury to deal with the causative agent and to remove dead cells and other rubbish by phagocytosis. Pus, frequently seen in acute inflammation is a mixture of dead cells, cell debris, fibrin, inflammatory exudate and living and dead microbes. Eventually the pus and or rubbish is removed paving the way for healing to begin. Resolution is complete when the inflammatory process is reversed, damaged cells having been phagocytosed, fibrin strands broken down, waste material removed by the blood and lymph and the injury has been repaired.

Abscesses and ulcers

OK so now we know what happens initially, before healing has commenced, when the skin becomes compromised. What are we actually going to see? Well the most obvious external symptom and indication of infection would be an abscess. We have established that redness will be present but we may not be able to see this. Certainly there will be some degree of heat and there may also be noticeable swelling depending on the severity of trauma/damage. There is also likely to be some element of pain as the exudate causes pressure on the sensory nerve endings.

An abscess is a localized pocket within a solid tissue containing a purulent exudate that is thick and yellow green in colour. They are formed when pus cannot drain out of an area of inflammation. We call this exudate pus and it is indicative of a bacterial infection of which the most common causes are the microbes *Staphylococcus aureus* and *Streptococcus pyogenes*. Superficial abscesses have a tendency to rupture and discharge their contents onto the surface of the skin. This process is followed by healing and unless there is extensive tissue damage is usually complete and without scarring. Deep-seated abscesses are a rather different matter that can have a number of outcomes.

- The abscess may burst and discharge its contents onto the surface of the skin. This, as we have seen, is followed by healing.

- The abscess may burst and discharge part of its contents onto the surface of the skin. This is followed by development of a chronic abscess with formation of an infected open channel known as a sinus.

- The abscess may burst into adjacent tissue or existing cavity forming an infected channel open at either end called a fistula.

- The abscess may not burst but the infective material and debris is removed by phagocytes and the abscess then heals.

Ulcers form when the superficial inflamed tissue sloughs off the surface of the skin leaving an open sore. This can cause problem with healing where the circulation is poor. Ulcers may become quite deep and can enlarge into a cavity. When healing takes place it is by second intention.

The Skin Healing Process

The skin has the most amazing ability to repair itself when damaged and in fact the rate at which the skin heals can be a barometer as to general well-being. Before effective wound healing can take place a number of conditions need to be met including good nutritional status and general health. The healing process can be retarded by factors such as low immunity, infection and poor blood supply and is also affected by some conditions such anaemia. A good blood supply bringing nutrients and oxygen to the site of the injury and removing waste products and debris will greatly facilitate wound healing as will freedom from any kind of contamination. Contaminants could be foreign bodies, bacteria or toxic chemicals. Other factors that can delay healing include reduced cell division (mitosis) due to advanced age, dehydration and excessive movement.

The healing process is kicked off initially by damage to the skin involving some level of destruction of tissue. This damage can be minimal, for example a graze, or involve more extensive destruction of tissue. The circulatory system round which the blood flows is basically a sealed system from which any leakage is treated by the body as a serious matter requiring an immediate response.

When the integrity of the skin is breached, that is damage occurs, a sequence of events begins in which the skin is restored to its normal or near normal structure and function. Depending on the extent of the injury two types of wound healing can occur, epidermal wound healing where only the superficial layers of the skin are involved and deep wound healing where damage has been done to the dermis and subcutaneous layers and possibly underlying structures. These two types are known as primary and secondary healing or healing by first intention and healing by second intention.

Blood Clot Formation

As we have already said the circulatory system is a sealed system and any breach will instigate the formation of a blood clot. Clotting is a complex

Skin healing process

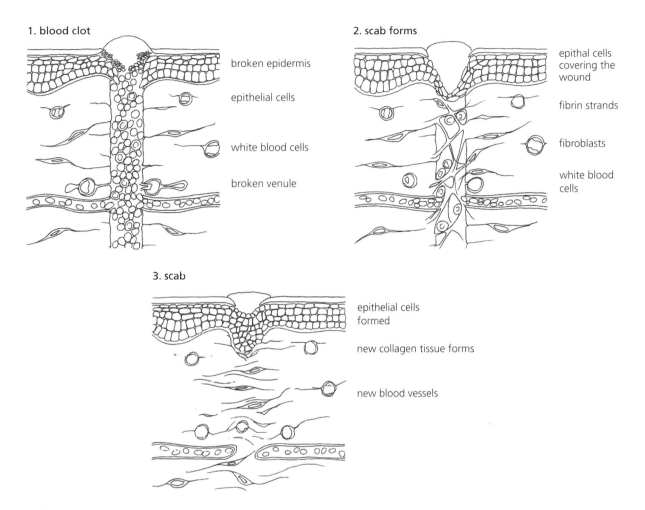

1. blood clot

broken epidermis

epithelial cells

white blood cells

broken venule

2. scab forms

epithal cells covering the wound

fibrin strands

fibroblasts

white blood cells

3. scab

epithelial cells formed

new collagen tissue forms

new blood vessels

process that moves through a series of defined steps from start to finish, it is therefore said to be stepwise. Being stepwise and complex reduces the risk of clots forming where they are not wanted in undamaged vessels.

The process begins when there is some loss of blood. Platelets, a cellular component of blood, become damaged and tissue is exposed to higher levels of oxygen than it would normally be. The correct name for platelets is thrombocytes, thrombus meaning clot. Loss of blood, damaged platelets and an increase in oxygen leads to the release of thromboplastins from the platelets. Thromboplastins along with vitamin K and calcium ions in the blood cause inactive prothrombin to change to active thrombin. The presence of thrombin causes soluble fibrinogen to convert to insoluble fibrin which exists as protein fibres that form a mesh or net over the wound. Finally the mesh traps red blood cells (erythrocytes) creating a plug of cells that then dries out to produce a scab. Having stopped the leak as it were the next stage of healing can begin.

Epidermal Wound Healing

This type of healing takes place when the damage is minimal and the edges of the wound are in close proximity. In some cases the wound may extend into the dermis. A common type of this kind of skin damage is an abrasion or graze where the surface of the skin has been scraped away, in this case the superficial epidermal cells have sustained only slight damage at the edges of the wound and the epidermal cells migrate across the wound from the edges. Once the migration is complete and the wound is covered the cells divide and move upwards until the normal thickness of skin is restored. Scar tissue is not usually formed.

Primary Healing

Stage 1

As we discovered earlier, a blood clot and cell debris fills the gap between the cut surfaces. Inflammation, an integral part of the healing process, develops around the damaged area.

Stage 2

Special cells called phagocytes begin to 'eat up' the blood clot and cell debris and granulation tissue starts to grow into the gap. Granulation tissue is moist and pink in colour and is very fragile being easily broken down by microorganisms or trauma. Whilst this is going on epithelial basal cells detach from the basement membrane and migrate across the wound. These cells advance in a sheet until cells migrating from the opposite direction are encountered. The migration finally stops when all the basal cells are in contact with another basal cell. The halting of the migration is due to a cellular response called contact inhibition.

Stage 3

The blood clot has now been completely removed and the scab becomes detached.

Stage 4

The thickness of the skin is restored by layers of epithelial cells growing upwards to produce new strata and the wound is healed.

Stage 5

Fibrous tissue continues to grow strengthening the edges of the wound.

Stage 6

Finally the inflammation resolves leaving scar tissue.

Generally stage two takes between three and five days, the final stages advance concurrently and take between two and four weeks.

Deep wound healing

This process is more complex due to the multiple layers of tissue that must be repaired. Healing progresses in four phases. In deep wound healing some of the tissue function is lost and scar tissue is formed.

Inflammatory phase

In this phase the blood clot forms to fill the wound and join the edges. Inflammation helps to eliminate infection and deal with any foreign and dying material in the wound by increasing the delivery of white blood cells to the site of injury. The following three phases do the work of repairing the injury.

Migratory phase

During this phase the clot scabs over and the epithelial cells migrate across the wound to bridge the gap. Synthesization of scar tissue begins and damaged blood vessels start to re-grow. At this point the tissue filling the wound is granulation tissue.

Proliferative phase

Under the scab extensive growth of epithelial cells takes place along with random deposition of fibres. Blood vessel growth continues.

Maturation phase

Once the epidermis has attained normal thickness the scab sloughs off. Fibres that have been deposited at random previously now become more organized and blood vessels are returned to normal.

Scar Tissue (Fibrosis)

Having looked at the processes of healing it is important we understand the nature and development of scar tissue. By its very nature scar tissue will have an impact on the function of a tissue. Deep wound healing of the skin sometimes results in the formation of a scar raised above the level of the normal epidermis. In addition scar tissue is likely to contain fewer hair follicles, sweat glands, blood vessels and nerve endings than undamaged skin. In scar tissue the collagen fibres are more densely packed and this coupled with less blood vessels results in scars being lighter in colour than normal skin. Scar tissue is formed when normal healing takes place but there is loss of tissue or the damaged cells fail to regenerate. Granulation tissue forms and over time the inflammatory and other material is removed leaving only the collagen fibres. In the wrong place fibrous tissue can have long lasting and damaging effects. Over time scar tissue shrinks and this can be especially problematic across joints as it inevitably will restrict movement.

4.

Examination of the Skin

Watch, listen, learn.

The Importance of Examination

In terms of that old adage being 'forewarned is forearmed', paying close attention to your horse's skin is very important. From the point of view of your horse's health the first indications of illness or disease are likely to manifest themselves in some way in the skin. Early identification of an impending problem will make that problem much easier to deal with.

Initially the best way to tackle this is to make an observation checklist that you can run through as you deal with your horse. This list will involve observations using three of your five senses and after a while it will become second nature as you develop a sort of sixth sense about the health status of your horse. A horse with a harsh staring coat is definitely not at his best neither is one with a yellow tinge to the sclera of the eye, in both cases the cause needs to be investigated. The secret of effective examination is a case of tuning up the senses and trusting yourself. If you spot something that you think is not quite right you are, in all probability, correct and not just being fanciful. After all, if it does turn out to be your imagination nothing is lost but it could be very different if an early warning signal is ignored.

Although it may seem very obvious one of the most important reasons for examining the skin as a whole is to make sure that it is intact. Cuts and abrasions, even small, insignificant ones, allow the invasion of bacteria which could possibly lead to infection. As you can imagine this can be disastrous near a joint.

Because of the coat we are not always able to see very minor breaks in the skin and for that reason it is vital that you keep your horse's tetanus cover up to date. Tetanus, or lockjaw as it is also known, is a bacteria that normally lives in the soil. It can get into the system through the tiniest graze although the horse is most at risk from deep puncture wounds or those that are not exposed to the air. Once a horse has been infected symptoms are caused by a toxin released by the bacteria, this toxin spreads through the body affecting the nervous system. Almost all cases of tetanus are fatal, those animals that do survive have, in all probability, been caught very early on following infection. Horses and ponies are the most susceptible of the domestic animals but humans can also contract the disease so keep your own tetanus cover up to date. Where there is no obvious site of infection the disease is referred to as 'idiopathic tetanus' but as sure as eggs are eggs there will be a breach in the skin somewhere.

It is also important that we examine the skin for signs of parasites such as lice. These must be dealt with promptly as they are stealing nourishment from your horse and in the past I have seen horses that were reduced to skin and bone by a heavy external parasitic infestation.

As I mentioned earlier, when we examine the skin we need to use all our senses including our sense of smell. Get to know what your horse's own smell is like and again trust your judgment if you think the smell has changed. Toxins produced as a result of disease are frequently eliminated through the skin and can change what the horse smells like.

Finally our sense of touch as an instrument of examination is extremely useful. Frequently warmth can be felt in an area before other signs of disease manifest themselves allowing for early remedial action. Touch also allows us to detect and evaluate pain and to appraise muscular tension. Changes in the texture of the coat can alert us to the early stages of some skin diseases and we will look at these in more detail in the chapter on condition and disease of the skin.

Having considered all of the above it becomes obvious what a valuable aid examination of the skin is in our effort to maintain our horses in optimum health.

Visual Examination of the Skin and Coat

To start with you should be familiar with and be able to recognize the signs of health. As we have seen in earlier chapters there are a number of clear signs that a horse is healthy and these are not hard to spot. The first of these is a sleek and glossy coat. This indicates that the skin has a good blood supply carrying plenty of oxygen and nutrients to the tissues. Oils secreted in the sebum lubricates the surface of the skin and imparts a sheen to the coat. The horse is comfortable with the surrounding temperature and is not cold so the hair of the coat is lying flat against the skin. There will be no signs of sweating, no visible swellings or puffiness and no cuts or abrasions. Finally the membranes around the eye and inside the nostrils should be moist and a good pink colour.

There are plenty of visual signs that all is not well with the horse. The most obvious of these is a coarse, staring coat that has a dull appearance and feels dry. Similarly excessive amounts of scurf in the coat are not a good sign although this could be due to a poor grooming regime. Sweating not related to exercise can indicate that the horse is in pain and puffy limbs are symptoms of a number of illnesses.

Look out for patchy hair loss as this might be ringworm – a very contagious skin condition – whilst a horse that does not shed his coat might have Cushing's disease.

Scars, though not strictly a sign of ill health, tell us something about a horse's previous medical history. In real terms they mean the horse has sustained some level of injury in the past which may or may not be significant, they also serve as a means of identification as they are permanent and cannot be removed.

Freeze marks are also highly visible and are meant to be so to discourage theft. Some insurance companies will give a discount for horses that are freeze marked but for obvious reasons freeze marking is useless on light greys.

Flat Hand Exploration

Many people, other than giving the horse a desultory pat when he has done well and running hands down the legs to check for lumps, bumps and heat, only touch their horses with a brush and never with their bare hands. Believe me, both they and their horse are missing out.

As with people, some horses need to get used to being touched in an intimate way, they have their own 'space' which some do not like to be invaded. Respect this space and ask to be allowed into it as forcibly invading it can do more harm than good.

Flat hand exploration is exactly what it says it is, exploration of the horse's body with the flat of the bare hand. It is a great technique for getting to know your horse and establishing a relationship and practised carefully it will help build trust and aid relaxation. In addition to the bonding aspect of this technique a lot can be learnt about your horse, not only about his skin and the condition of the underlying structures, but about his mental state of mind and how he responds to an intimate touch in what is in fact, after all, an invasion of his personal space. Carried out on a regular basis flat hand exploration can

1. Start your examination on the neck, behind the horse's ears, or as near to it as he will allow. Allow the full weight of the hand to rest on the skin without exerting pressure and move smoothly and slowly down the neck towards the withers. Make a note of any spots that feel hotter or cooler than the surrounding skin or that feel hard and tense. For the first pass I like to work all along the top line and down the outside of the hind leg as this corresponds to the line of the bladder meridian, however you may choose to work across the head, neck and shoulders before moving down the back.

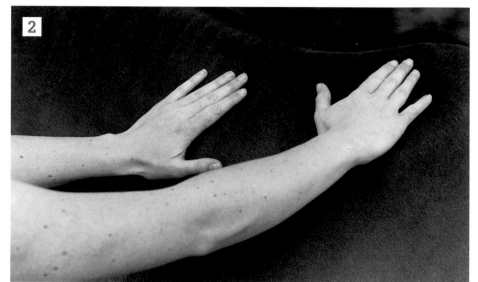

2. A good relaxed flat hand contact, moving down the neck and over the withers.

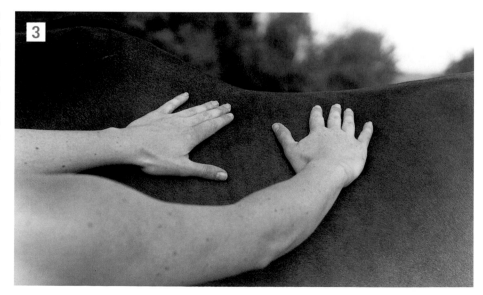

3. Continue along the back, pay particular attention to the saddle area in case there are areas of tension caused by ill-fitting tack or poor rider position. Make sure your hands remain relaxed.

4. Still relaxed and with an even pressure, continue over the rump. After a while the horse will begin to relax under the hands and enjoy the sensation of this kind of touch. Indications that he is relaxing are sighing, drooping eyelids and lower lip, licking the lips and lowering the head.

5. If possible the pressure and rate of progress should be consistent all the way through the procedure. It is very helpful to have an assistant who can mark areas of hot or cold or changes in texture on a diagram but if you are not lucky enough to have one you will need to stop and mark these on the chart yourself. Initially, keeping a record of your flat hand exploration is very important from the point of view of recognising changes.

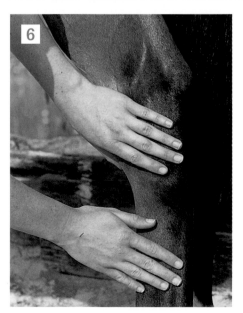

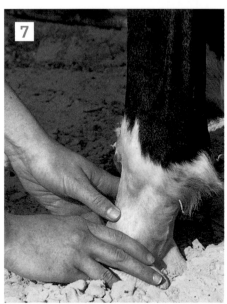

6. Moving down the hind leg. Frequently the temperature of the leg changes below the hock or knee. This is usually due to the subtle energies being blocked.

7. Finally check the temperature of the hoof and pastern before slowly withdrawing the hands.

alert you to changes that may indicate a health or well-being problem in the offing.

Initially you may wonder what exactly you are looking for, or more accurately, feeling for, but don't be put off, after the first couple of times when your hands have become more 'educated' you'll become familiar with the temperature and texture of your horse's coat making it much easier to spot changes. Using your hands in this way will also allow you to get to know the condition of the underlying muscles, relaxed muscle feels quite different to muscle tissue in spasm which feels different again to bone.

To begin the process of tactile familiarization for your hands have a practice with various articles from around the house or yard. A gel pad wrapped in a duster gives a good representation of what relaxed muscle will feel like whilst a tennis ball feels more like muscle in tension. Your own shinbone will give you a good idea of what a bony ridge feels like. Small screwtop bottles of the sort used for fizzy drinks can be used to help with temperature appreciation by filling them with water of differing temperatures and covering again with a duster or some other kind of fluffy cloth.

Before you begin a flat hand exploration make sure you have a safe, secure place to carry out the procedure that is comfortable for both you and the horse. A well lit, roomy box that the horse is familiar with, though not necessarily his own stable, is ideal. If you can find an assistant so much the better but if not make sure you have a good place to tie up and let somebody know what you are doing. Take the time to have a good look at the horse. At this point you can carry out a thorough visual examination if you have time but in any event look out for patches of scurfy skin, areas of hair loss, dull staring coat etc. It is a good idea to record your observations to build up a comprehensive set of notes.

First make a note of any areas of the coat that are coarse or raised and dull or that give the appearance of being lifeless. A template diagram similar to that used to record identification marks when a horse is vetted can be use to record your findings. Make sure you note down the date and time of day you carried out the examination. Also record any new scars your horse has acquired since the last time as these will need to be added to his ID at some time in the future. Sniff the coat, yes I know it sounds daft, and think about how he smells to you, his own personal smell may change when he is ill so it is a good idea to know what he smells like when he is well.

Having employed your eyes and your nose we can begin the flat hand exploration but before we do you need to prepare yourself. Unfortunately any tension or anxiety you may be feeling can easily be transmitted to the horse so you need to calm and ground yourself. Take time to take a few deep breaths and relax before approaching the horse. Place both hands on the horse, palms down so that the whole of the hand, including the fingers, is in contact with the coat. If the horse moves away from you try again and either reduce or

A patch of raised hair in an otherwise good coat. The coat in this area could be rough for any number of reasons, in this case the horse had banged her leg a few days earlier and the area was probably bruised.

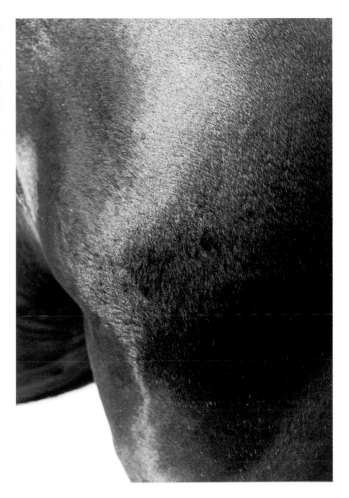

increase the pressure of your hand but don't force him into acceptance. Start at the head of the horse behind the ear, or as close to it as the horse will allow, and run your palm down the neck just under (about three inches) where the mane hair starts to grow. Continue down the flank, over the rump and down the hind leg to the foot. Note the temperature of the skin and coat, particularly any hot or cold spots and record these on your chart. Also make a note of places where the tightness of the skin and texture of the hair varies and the places touched where the horse fidgets and begins to move around. Repeat this exercise in lines parallel to the original sweep until you have covered the whole of one side of the horse, finally finishing of with the front leg. Having done one side, don't forget to do the other.

OK so what are we looking for? The horse should have a uniform temperature all over his body so a hot or cold spot is generally an indication of some kind of interference in the energy flow. In traditional Chinese medicine this energy is also known as chi. Excess or depletion of chi leads to hot or cold spots respectively, any variations in temperature should be marked on the chart.

The skin should move easily over the underlying tissue and should not feel stiff and immobile. In horses that are sick the skin frequently tightens up resulting in the expression 'hidebound'. Test an area of skin behind the elbow for 'tenting' as this may be a sign of dehydration. In a horse that is in the peak of health the hair of the mane should be quite hard to pull out, if the mane pulls out easily there may be something wrong.

As you become more proficient with flat hand exploration your horse will begin to relax more and more early on in the procedure. Watch out for sighing which is a sure sign of tension release. He may also lower his head and relax the lower lip. Eventually his eyelids will droop and he will be almost asleep.

Veterinary Examination

Apart from the usual visual and tactile examination a vet does they may also elect to carry out more detailed laboratory procedures. There is a great deal to be learned from microscopic examination of material collected from the hair and the surface of the skin and because of its accessibility this is relatively easy.

Ectoparasites can be obtained using skin scrapings or acetate tape impressions and hair and exudate can be collected and examined. Skin biopsy is a very powerful tool in the diagnosis of a disease or condition but needs to be performed with precision and attention to detail if it is to be of any value.

Acetate Tape Impressions

Used as an alternative to skin scrapings to find superficial parasites such as lice or mites. The sticky side of the tape is pressed onto the hairs and the skin next to parted hair. It may be necessary to shave the area. Scales of dead skin and debris are collected on the tape which is stuck onto a microscope slide and examined.

Skin Scrapings

Skin scrapings are also used for the detection of parasites. It is a simple procedure and can be superficial or deep depending on the type of parasite that is expected to be found. The sample is taken by using a surgical blade to scrape the surface of the skin onto a laboratory slide and fixing it with a cover.

Hair Examination

Hairs are plucked from the area to be investigated and examined under a microscope. Hair examination can reveal nutritional or metabolic disorders.

Cytologic Examination

This procedure uses microscopic examination of smears of tissues and fluids collected from skin lesions. It is used to detect the presence of fungi and bacteria. There are a number of different methods of material collection including swabs, fine needle aspiration, impression and direct smears. The collected material is transferred to a slide, allowed to dry and stained before examination under a microscope.

Biopsy

Properly performed skin biopsy can lead to a correct diagnosis in ninety per cent of dermatological cases but it does not replace a proper physical examination and only adds information. It is important when selecting a site to biopsy that a macule, pustule or lesion is centred in the biopsy specimen.

5.

Maintenance of Healthy Skin

Avoiding Coat and Skin Problems

There are many factors that affect the health of your horse's skin including environment, nutrition, health status and external influences creating stress. The skin, as we have seen earlier is very resilient and capable of repairing itself but eventually, if it is consistently challenged, the structure will weaken and it will become more susceptible to disease. To keep the skin in optimum condition we need to avoid these challenging factors and to avoid them we need first to understand them.

Improving and maintaining the health of your horse's skin involves keeping it clean by regular and appropriate grooming, nurturing it with a good plane of nutrition, adequate hydration and avoiding stressful or damaging situations. We will investigate the nourishment and hydration of the skin in the chapter on 'Nutrition for a Healthy Skin', which is a subject all on its own, but we also need to consider situations which lead to skin damage and strategies for keeping the skin clean.

Skin Stress

Stress can be put on the skin in any number of ways from muddy, inadequate conditions to continuous trauma. Some of these can easily be avoided whilst others may have to be endured.

The easiest stress to avoid it that which is imposed by equipment and clothing, that means making sure your tack not only fits the horse properly but is supple and clean at all times and that the rugs are the right size, are clean and don't rub. Dirty or ill-fitting tack is the cause of all sorts of stress both physical and mental. It can abrade the skin and lead to varying levels of pain and discomfort that will ultimately predispose disease and allow the invasion of pathogens.

Another cause of stress that will eventually affect the skin is unsuitable living conditions. This is not always so easy to deal with and unfortunately in some circumstances you may need to compromise. Wet weather can create muddy conditions, which you may have no control over especially if your horse has to live out. In this case extra vigilance is needed to avoid diseases such as mud rash and if it becomes very muddy or your horse shows signs of developing the disease it would be worthwhile considering moving him to alternative accommodation. Some horse owners will face similar problems in the summer, not as the result of muddy conditions, but because of the culcoides midge, the primary cause of sweet itch. In fact anything that stresses the horse will stress the skin.

These two horses have found a way to indulge in mutual grooming despite each having their own paddock and being separated by post and rail fencing. This highlights how important it is for horses to be able to touch each other if only to carry out necessary, social activities like this.

Preventing Physical Skin Damage

Wherever you keep your horse you need to check for rough surfaces and protrusions that can physically damage your horse's skin. This includes barbed wire, which is regrettably used in many places for fencing as it is cheap and effective but is far from suitable for horses. Barbed wire can, especially if it is

This fencing is in a very bad state of repair, the wood is old and split, there is barbed wire along the top and, in the centre of the picture, a six inch nail is sticking out of the fence.

left lying around, inflict severe damage even to the extent of necessitating the humane destruction of the animal and apart from inflicting ragged tears in the horse's skin will also damage his rugs. Where old wire is left lying around there is a very real risk of the horse becoming tangled up in it and the staples attaching the wire to the posts can easily pierce the foot if they become dislodged and fall into the grass.

If the field where your horse grazes is fenced with barbed wire you can minimize the risk to him by regular inspections to ensure the posts are not loose and that the wire still has the correct tension. Even better still a strand of electric fencing run around the inside about two feet from the barbed wire will offer extra protection and although it won't remove the risk completely it will considerably lessen it.

The best type of fencing for horses is post and rail but this can be just as dangerous as barbed wire if it is not maintained in good condition. The posts should be firm in the ground and the rails in one piece and not tied together with bailer twine, in fact a horse can too easily be impaled on a broken rail or injured by a nail that is not hammered down.

The best way to keep your horse safe when he is out grazing is to regularly and methodically check his field for anything that might injure him. People have a nasty habit of throwing rubbish over fences, this can include old tin cans and broken glass, not to mention fly-tipping of broken down refrigerators, bedsteads and old cars none of which make for a very healthy environment. Once you get into the habit of checking the fences and have tuned your eye to spot any potentially harmful rubbish your horse is less likely to be injured whilst out in the field.

Barbed wire is bad enough at any time but putting a horse in a paddock with fencing in this condition is asking for trouble.

Temporary electric fencing dividing a paddock. Electric fencing of this sort works very well with horses as they very soon learn to respect it. It can be used to restrict or control grazing safely and effectively.

The broken top rail of this post and rail fence needs to be replaced as soon as possible.

A good example of a clean and healthy grazing environment with a good selection of natural herbage. The horse in the foreground is wearing a fly net and mask.

Having inspected the grazing and satisfied yourself that there is nothing that your horse can injure himself on go on to apply equal vigilance to the stable. Look for any projections such as nails or screws that the horse can catch himself on or loose boards and sagging door that could do with attention. Make sure the roof is sound and not leaking and check that the stable drains properly and that foul waste and liquid does not accumulate at the back.

There are some horses that don't like rats and as most stables will attract them this can cause a problem. Whilst the rats themselves are not usually a problem, their scurryings and scratching can easily upset (stress) a sensitive horse. Rats are most active at night when there is nobody about and their machinations will undoubtedly disturb your horse's rest.

Short of sitting up at night you will probably never see them but there will be tell-tale signs that they are there. Look for holes in the bedding banks at the back in both corners but the biggest indication of their presence is a restless horse. If your horse has previously been clean in the stable but has taken to churning up his bed at night he is likely to be being disturbed by rats. Keeping them out of a stable, once they have established a run through it, is not that easy and you might want to move to another stable if there is one available. Failing that, make sure all the holes are blocked up and keep them that way.

To conclude, preventing physical skin damage means having clean tack and clothing that fits properly, ensuring that there are no objects, fences, nails or other items that the horse could damage himself on out in his field, making sure his stable is a warm, dry comfortable place for him to sleep that is free from draughts and vermin and taking care to maintain things properly. Having done all of this you can rest easy in the knowledge that you have done everything you could to prevent breaching the integrity of the skin.

Cleaning the Skin

Cleaning the skin for a horse is very important and can be done by us or by mutual grooming by other horses. The surface film of normal skin contains a number of things including, dead skin cells, the excreted products of the skin glands, dirt, pollen, mould spores and bacteria. Abnormal skin surface film contains excessive amounts of these along with a wide variety of substances such as exudates, serum and degenerated cells and their by-products.

Shifting that little lot so that the skin can remain healthy is done by grooming and if this is neglected you can soon run into trouble. Problems can also be encountered from the use of hair care products such as shampoos and conditioners, especially if the horse has skin that is sensitive to some of the contents.

Shampoos, and there are numerous brands on the market, should remove dirt and grease from the skin and coat leaving it soft and shiny. They must be easy to rinse out and leave no residue behind on the surface of the skin. Ideally shampoos should just remove the dirt and debris but in practice they usually also remove the oils needed for warmth and protection, from the horse's coat. This is not so important for a stabled horse but could be devastating for a horse or pony that is kept out all year round.

The horse's skin has a pH of 7 to 7.4 which is roughly neutral, and is different to human skin making pH adjusting shampoos recommended for people unsuitable for equine use. Although there is no research to back it up, it is likely that these pH products can temporarily alter the normal barrier functions of the skin making it more vulnerable to attack.

Shampoos are usually made of either soap or detergent. Soap-based shampoos are fine in areas of soft water but where the water is hard they have a tendency to leave a film on the hair making it dull looking. Detergent-based shampoos are much harsher although they do not produce different results if the water is hard or soft. Some horses can have an adverse reaction to some of the ingredients so you need to monitor this closely to make sure you do not irritate the horse's skin. Detergent shampoos tend to dry the coat so it is recommended that some kind of conditioner be used afterwards.

Topical Skin Therapy

Topical skin therapy delivers some form of 'medicine' directly onto the surface of the skin for the prevention or treatment of a variety of skin diseases. As the skin is the largest and most accessible organ in the body, topical therapy has always played a large role in the treatment of skin disorders.

Medicines for topical application consist of an active ingredient (drug) and a carrier of some kind, for example a cream or a lotion. The purpose of the carrier is to facilitate the application of the active ingredient onto the skin, or in some cases as with aloe vera gel, to deliver the ingredient into the deeper layers of the skin itself. In some instances the carrier may be totally inert and play no active part in the treatment being administered whilst in others it may have important therapeutic effects of its own.

The effectiveness of a drug when applied topically is frequently affected by absorption although this is not synonymous with the rate with which it is absorbed into the skin. A number of factors to do with the drug itself and its interaction with the carrier also play a large part in the efficacy of the treatment. When applied to the skin, to be effective, a drug must move from the carrier into the epidermis. The ability to do this will depend on the concentration and solubility of the drug in the carrier and the penetrative qualities of the carrier itself. Drugs that are fat soluble penetrate the skin barrier more readily than others that are not, this is because the stratum corneum itself is lipophilic or in common parlance 'fat loving'. From this we can see that the amount of a drug taken into the skin depends on three different interactions, those between the drug and the carrier, between the drug and the skin and between the carrier and the skin. Increased solubility and delivery of the drug can have systemic effects, in other words an effect on the whole body, which is potentially dangerous, this applies particularly to corticosteroids applied in an ointment base carrier.

Other variables that affect absorption are temperature and level of hydration, the latter more so than the former. As a rule the permeability of the skin increases with the level of hydration of the stratum corneum so if your horse is dehydrated the effectiveness of any topically applied medication will be reduced.

The health and condition of the skin also contributes to the uptake of medication. Inflammation, abrasions and other kinds of damage will increase the quantity of drug absorbed as will an increase in blood supply to the skin.

Active Ingredients

Active ingredients fall into several categories. These are:

- **Antifungal** For treating fungal infections such as ringworm.

- **Antibacterial** An antibiotic for treating bacterial infections such as infected cuts.

- **Antiseptic** A chemical that inhibits the growth of bacteria and other micro-organisms that is gentle enough to be applied to the skin and mucous membranes. Used to cleanse wounds and prevent infections.

- **Antiparasitic** For dealing with ectoparasites such as lice.

- **Anti-inflammatory** Used to reduce inflammation. Depending on the type of anti-inflammatory, these act against one or more of the mediators that initiate or maintain the inflammatory response.

- **Antiseborrheic** To stop the excess production of sebum by the sebaceous glands leading to the condition seborrhoea.

- **Antipruritic** For relieving and soothing itchy conditions.

- **Astringents** Drying agents. Used in lotions to harden and protect the skin and also to reduce bleeding from minor cuts and abrasions.

- **Emollient** To sooth and soften the skin. They can be used alone as moisturisers or in skin preparations as a base for a more active drug.

- **Ultraviolet screens** To prevent sunburn.

Applications

There are a number of different ways of delivering the active ingredients to the skin with the system used dictated by the lesion or disease being treated however, the same active ingredient may be available in a number of different formulations and methods of delivery. In order to facilitate contact with the skin it may be necessary to clip the hair, this will maximize the benefit of the product.

Shampoos

Medicated shampoos have active ingredients added to them to either enhance the properties of the shampoo or add new ones. They are not usually in contact with the skin for very long so have limited application although they are very useful for treating large areas of the body or for localized problems. Medicated shampoos are used extensively for treating external parasitic infections such as fleas and lice. Delivering medication by this method usually requires that the product be left on the skin for a certain length of time before it is rinsed off. This needs to be timed quite carefully but usually fifteen minutes is enough as this also allows for some hydration of the stratum corneum. To gain full benefit it may also be necessary to de-grease the skin before a medicated shampoo is used. For this wash with a baby shampoo or washing-up liquid to remove the dirt and debris from the coat and skin.

Horses that are washed frequently or that have skins that are on the dry side are in danger of losing the oils from their coats so choose a shampoo that is hypoallergenic and contains moisturisers.

Conditioners are slightly acidic which has the effect of hardening up the keratin from which the hair is composed. They reduce static electricity and provide body to limp hair, they can also replenish the oils lost when shampooing and, because they are rarely completely removed, can be used to deliver medication to the skin.

Rinses

Rinses are a good way of treating large areas of skin. They are made by mixing an active ingredient, such as a concentrated liquid or soluble powder, with water. They can then be poured, sponged or sprayed onto the horse.

Lotions

Lotions are liquids in which an active ingredient, such as a powder, is dissolved or suspended. They can have a water or alcohol base which makes them more drying than liniments that have an oily base. They have a variety of applications and are used to carry various active ingredients.

Powders

Powders are made by finely grinding organic or inorganic matter. They are applied to the skin in a thin coat, dissolved in water to form a rinse, added to other liquids to make a lotion or to creams or ointments to form pastes. Because they can build up and can be inhaled, powders are not a popular method of delivering medication although they are commonly used for the control of skin parasites and as an antiseptic wound powder to treat small areas. The efficacy of both these treatments depends largely on the way they are applied.

Sprays

Used to treat large areas of the coat or small areas without hair. Sprays are frequently used to apply fly repellents, astringents, anti-inflammatories or moisturisers.

Creams and ointments

Creams and ointments are used to hold medication in intimate contact with the skin. They can be occlusive thereby preventing water loss from the surface of the skin and have smoothing and lubricating properties.

Gels

Gels mix readily with water and can be used to transport any active ingredient mixed into them directly into the skin. They are non greasy and when rubbed in do not leave a sticky film on the surface making them better tolerated than creams and ointments.

Hydrotherapy

The therapeutic properties of water are frequently overlooked especially as it is commonly used in lotions, rinses and shampoos. On its own water can be used to cool or warm the skin, to soften any surface crusts and to clean. Depending on how it is used hydrotherapy can hydrate or dehydrate the skin. Mostly water is employed before other medications are applied.

Physical Therapy

Using heat and cold as a physical skin therapy is not new and the benefits of both have been known for centuries. Treatment using light and radiation is more recent but still not that new, however in the past few years advances have been made in all these therapies which have made them more specific so much so that freezing, electricity, lasers and heat are now commonly used as surgical techniques.

Magnetic therapy using biomagnets supposedly increases the circulation

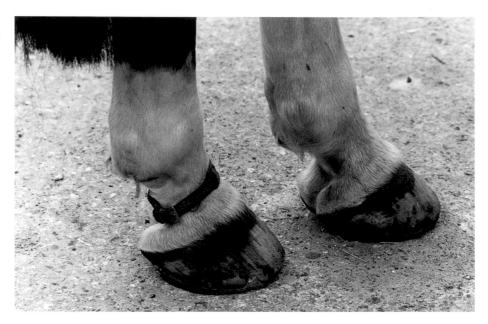

A leather covered, copper anklet worn to provide subtle energy therapy for arthritis.

and causes warming locally although this has not been proved in horses. However ultrasound did cause local warming.

Mutual Grooming

Horses in the wild are not subject to a great many skin diseases and usually have lovely glossy coats but this is obviously not due to the attentions of any grooms. Wild or feral horses must therefore find some other way to keep their coats in pristine condition and their skins free from parasites but we would be quite wrong in assuming they are never groomed. Wild horses in a herd groom each other and we call this mutual grooming. Mutual grooming is part of a horse's natural, social behaviour, by virtue of its intimacy it strengthens bonds between individuals in the herd and quite literally is a case of you scratch my back and I'll scratch yours. If you take the time to observe horses out at grass together, especially in the summer months you will see examples of mutual grooming, the horses standing nose to tail chewing away at each others' manes and backs. With this simple, natural act they keep their skins and coats in optimum condition by using their teeth and lips to dislodge and remove scurf and parasites.

This sort of social interaction is very important to the horse's welfare but unfortunately many horses and ponies are denied this simple basic and to them necessary pleasure because they are too valuable to be allowed out with other horses. If we are not about to let our horses groom each other we must do it for them.

Mutual grooming. This helps to keep the coat and skin clean and healthy, note how the bay pony is using his lips and teeth on the neck of the chestnut pony who is obviously reciprocating.

Equipment

In order to keep your horse's skin clean and free from parasites and in good condition you will need a least a basic grooming kit. This consists of a range of brushes and other bits and pieces for removing dirt of one kind and another from the horse's coat and skin and like any other tools you need to know how to use them properly to get the best effect. Grooming takes time and effort but the upside of this is that regular, thorough grooming goes a long way to maintaining health.

Basic Grooming Kit

Dandy brush

A hard backed-brush with stiff, medium length bristles of either natural or manmade fibres. This is used for removing surface dirt and debris like mud and bits of bedding adhering to the coat. It can be used all over the body except the more sensitive areas such as the face and around the udder or sheath and the main and tail. The dandy brush is gripped in the hand and is the best brush to use on a horse when they come in from the field. It is not designed as a deep cleaning brush and on fine skinned horses may prove to be too harsh. Used on the mane and tail it may break the hairs and its use for this purpose is therefore not recommended on show animals.

Body brush

This brush has shorter, softer and denser bristles than a dandy brush which may be made of natural or manmade fibres, it usually has a leather or soft plastic back. Generally a body brush is wider than a dandy brush and has a strap across the back through which to slip the hand. It therefore sits in the palm of the hand when in use and is usually not gripped by the fingers. The bristles of a body brush can range from relatively stiff to very fine and soft and prices are cheap to very expensive. Some horses can only bear to be brushed with very soft brushes and you should take your horse's needs into consideration when purchasing body brushes. The very best brushes usually have leather backs and pure hogs' bristle 'bristles', they can cost as mush as ten times that of a cheap range. The body brush is designed for deep cleaning of the coat and skin. It is also the only brush that should be used on the mane or tail.

Curry comb

There are many different designs of curry comb but they generally fall into two categories, those used directly on the horse and those not used on the horse. The latter are used to clean the body brush and consist of a handle attached to a rectangular metal plate with rows of teeth. The comb is drawn across the bristles of the body brush, at regular intervals during grooming, to remove dirt and

A basic grooming kit. *Clockwise from the left.* Grooming box with sponges, sweat scraper, blunt ended scissors, two sorts of curry comb, dandy brush, water brush, body brush, mane comb and hoof pick on a stable rubber, tail comb.

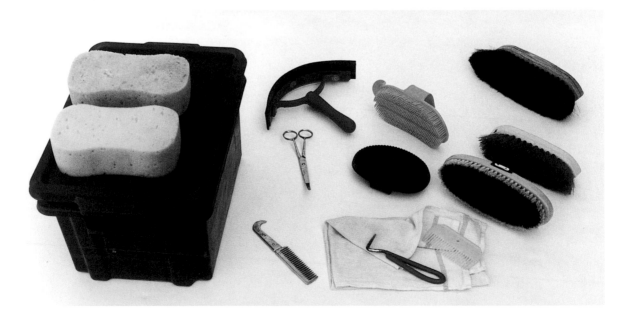

dead skin and then tapped on any convenient surface to clear the comb. Some metal curry combs have a strap across the back to slip you hand into instead of a handle.

The type of curry comb used directly on the horse is usually made of rubber with an integral strap across the back to slip the hand through much like a body brush. They are great for removing dead skin and hair from the coat and massaging the skin and can also be used to clean the body brush.

Water brush

A brush not unlike the dandy brush but smaller. Bristles are a little shorter than the dandy brush rather like a scrubbing brush. The water brush is used by dipping the tips of the bristles in clean water and slicking down the mane to lay it flat.

Main/tail combs

Made of either metal or plastic, these are for combing out the mane and tail but should only be used once they have been thoroughly brushed out with a body brush.

Hoof pick

Again there are a number of different designs of hoof pick on the market and all will do the same job. Some have stiff brushes set into the end of them for brushing loose dirt out of the hoof. When picking out a horse's feet the pick should always be used away from the body.

Stable rubber

These used to be made of linen but nowadays are usually a cotton mixture. They are exactly like kitchen tea towels and a kitchen tea towel will do just as well as a purpose-bought rubber. A stable rubber is used for giving a final polish to the coat following a full groom.

Sponges

You will need at least two of these and they are not interchangeable so it is as well to have them in different colours. Keep one for sponging the dock and sheath and another for cleaning the eyes and nostrils and both must be regularly washed in mild disinfectant and thoroughly rinsed.

Scissors

These should be blunt ended. Use for trimming hair from the head and legs.

Additional Equipment

Cactus cloth

A cactus cloth is made of openly woven rough natural fibres, it can also be bought made into a mitt with fleece on the reverse side. The cloth is very useful on a short coat for removing loose hairs and surface dirt. Used vigorously it is great for stimulating the skin. A horse with a very fine coat may prefer the use of a cactus cloth to a dandy brush.

Sweat scraper

There are a couple of different designs of sweat scraper for use either with one hand or two. The one-handed variety consists of a handle attached to a curved metal or plastic plate with a rubber edging, the scraper used with two hands is simply a long metal strip about two inches wide with a handle at either end.

Extra grooming kit. *Clockwise from the top.* Double handed strap sweat scraper, massaging curry comb, razor comb, leather backed body brush, soft bristled dandy brush, cactus cloth, metal curry comb for cleaning brushes, long bristled whisk brush.

As its name implies this piece of grooming equipment is used to remove excess water or sweat from the horse's coat.

Wisps

A real wisp is made of hay or straw that is twisted into a rope and then platted into a sausage-shaped pad that fits comfortably in the hand. Agricultural methods today mean that hay and straw is not usually long enough for making wisps. Alternatively a stuffed leather pad can be used for the same purpose. Whichever one you are using slap it hard onto the muscular areas of the neck, shoulders and rump, do not use on sensitive or bony areas. The purpose of wisping, or banging as it is also called, is to give the horse a muscle building massage. As the wisp is brought down onto the coat the horse will twitch in anticipation thus working the muscles. Wisping has largely gone out of fashion.

Mane drags

This is not an implement I would choose to use under any circumstances as in my opinion it spoils the horse's mane. Basically a mane drag is a comb with a blade that thins the mane as you comb it. It is the lazy man's way of pulling a mane.

Electrical Aids

Electric groomers

There are two sorts of electric groomers, rotary and suction. Both work extremely well and can save hours of slog if used once or twice a week. They are really little more than a small vacuum cleaner but care should be taken to keep the rotary type away from the horse's mane and tail.

Clippers

Electric clippers are used for taking off the coat as their name would suggest. The blades should be kept sharp and the motor regularly serviced.

Infra-red heater

An infra-red heater is very useful for drying and warming a wet horse. They are easy to install in the stable and cheap to run.

Grooming

There are significant benefits to be gained from grooming both for you and your horse not least of all the incredible difference you can make to his appearance. However not only does grooming help the horse to look good it also helps to keep them healthy. Parasites such as lice thrive on the dead skin and grease that can accumulate on the skin of an ungroomed horse and left undisturbed this provides the perfect nursery within which their young can thrive. It is also good practice to get into the habit of grooming your horse on a daily basis even if it is only a quick flick over with a brush – you will be much more likely to notice any recent injuries that may have been sustained and be able to treat them accordingly. One other benefit, if it is done properly, is that it will keep you fit.

Where do we start grooming a horse? I imagine that most of you have at least a nodding acquaintance with brushing a horse or pony but for those that haven't I'll start at the beginning.

There are a few preliminaries to observe before we can begin. The first thing to do is to assess what you are dealing with. If the horse has just come in from the field all muddy and wet he will need to dry off first before he can be groomed. It is very important that you do not start grooming a muddy, wet horse as this will only brush the mud into the coat instead of out of it. However there are a few things you can do to help him dry off more quickly before you start. I have always favoured a good rub down with a few handfuls of straw if you have any. Twist the straw into a pad, and briskly rub the horse all over the neck and body using a circular motion, avoid the bony bits as he may find it uncomfortable. This not only helps to dry the horse off and remove surface mud from the coat but also has the added advantage of stimulating the circulation to the skin and the tissues beneath it and of course will warm him up beautifully. Another trick is to put a layer of straw over the horse's back with a rug on top or if you don't have any straw to hand use a sweat rug in its place. You can of course just put a rug on the horse to keep him warm whilst he dries out but make sure it is the sort that wicks moisture away from the skin and doesn't seal it in. Whilst the horse dries off pick out his feet and brush his tail.

Now we have a dry horse we can begin. Start at the horse's head, behind the ears, the head will be groomed later on in the procedure. Select a dandy brush and brush with long sweeping strokes down the neck in the direction the hair is growing to remove any loose dirt or dried mud, this may not be necessary if your horse is stabled. Continue down the front leg, across the back and the flanks, over the rump and down the hind leg. Repeat all of this on the other side of the horse. Remembering the dandy brush has stiff bristles the pressure exerted should be enough to remove the surface dirt but not so much that the horse 'complains', equally your horse will not want to be tickled and you should take care in the more sensitive areas. Here I need to mention your own position and stance. The closer you are to the horse the better and safer you will be and the more power you can put behind your brush strokes; grooming properly is hard physical work.

Having removed all the loose dirt and mud now we come to the really hard work. Any stubborn stains can be sponged off (not with the face sponge) first before we start with the body brush. This bit is a two-handed operation, you will need the body brush in one hand and a curry comb in the other and the object of the exercise is to remove muck and debris from the skin. Start again with powerful long strokes down the neck in the same way we used the dandy brush. Every three or four strokes turn away from the horse and draw the brush across the teeth of the curry comb to remove loose hair and skin you have

Just in from the field, Sarah pushes the brush over Polo. The brush she is using is a relatively hard body brush as, being a Shire cross, Polo has quite a long, coarse coat even in summer. Finer skinned horses would probably object to being groomed with this sort of brush. Sarah could be standing a little closer to him than she is, this would give her more power behind her brush strokes with a corresponding deeper cleaning action.

brushed out of the coat. Every so often tap the curry comb on a hard surface to remove the dirt from that. In the olden days owners would look for little piles of dirt on the window ledge of their horse's stable to check that the groom was doing his job properly. The more you use the body brush the better for the condition of your horse's skin and coat but beware of using it too much on a grass-kept horse as it has a tendency to take the oils he needs to keep him warm out of the coat. Having completed the body brushing bit to your own satisfaction brush the tangles out of the main and tail and brush the face, again using the body brush. Having done this you should now have brushed your horse all over, including between the legs and under the mane and forelock. Next with a damp sponge clean the eyes and nostrils and with the other sponge clean the dock and, if you have a gelding, the sheath. Finally lay the mane with the water brush and give the coat a final polish with the stable rubber. Voila! Your horse is transformed. For an extra sheen to the coat wrap an old silk scarf, it must be pure silk and not synthetic, round a body brush and finish the coat with this.

As they age, horses develop a tendency to hang on to the winter coat in patches for longer than normal. The long hairs of the winter coat that has been imperfectly shed can be seen within the summer coat of this elderly horse.

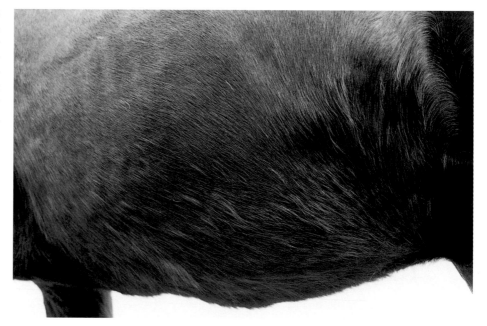

Hand Grooming

Hand grooming is one of the best ways I know of building trust and a relationship with your horse. It is a very intimate exercise with which he may well want to join in. Given the choice many horses would elect to be hand groomed as they dislike the feel of brushes on the skin but enjoy the intimacy of touch. There is no doubt that hand grooming produces the finest results but if you think grooming with a body brush is hard work hand grooming is even more so. With full-coated horses kept outside in winter it is not really very practical and for these purposes the hand is an inefficient way of getting rid of mud. However as a replacement for the body brush on a stabled horse it is excellent and there are numerous benefits to be had all round. Distinct advantages attach to grooming with the bare hand, the main one for the operative being that it is tantamount to a flat-hand exploration every time you groom in this way. You will be able to feel every lump and bump, every variation in texture of the coat, every difference in temperature of the skin and all the tensions of the muscles beneath the skin. In short it will tell you a lot about the mental and physical state of your horse's health. It will also tell you how clean he is. Apart from removing dirt this kind of all over stimulation will prod the skin glands to produce sebum which lubricates the skin and this along with the oil from your own hand, albeit a very minimal amount, will impart a wonderful gloss to the coat.

Provided it is approached in the right way and in the right frame of mind hand grooming will go a long way to calming a nervous and excitable animal as it stimulates relaxation in a way that conventional grooming does not. A few minutes into the procedure expect your horse to make a deep sigh as he relaxes in response to the comforting and rhythmical movements. Other signs of relaxation are lowering of the head and half closure of the eyes. Apart from the relaxation hand grooming brings it will also measurably increase the blood supply to the skin and underlying muscle, it is interesting to note that a hand placed on the skin will increase the blood supply to that area by eighty per cent. The overall effect of this is to increase the oxygen supply to the tissue, increase the nutrient supply to the cells and speed up the removal of toxins and waste products from cell respiration, all of which will have a beneficial affect on health.

The method of hand grooming is very similar to the use of the body brush in as much as you start at the neck, behind the ears and work in firm sweeping strokes down the neck. This kind of grooming is however something that invades personal space and some horses may initially not like such an intimate procedure so proceed carefully. Effectively what you are doing is stroking him all over.

Assuming your horse finds this kind of touch acceptable you can continue. If he fidgets or looks worried try doing a little at a time until he becomes used to this kind of handling. Take care to watch his body language as you move from one section to another, he might enjoy hand grooming in one place but dislike it in another and to gain maximum benefit from this exercise we must respect the horse's wishes.

Hand grooming can be done one or two handed but which ever way you choose try to build up a rhythm as this will help to relax the horse. Remember you are hand grooming and not delivering a massage so work firmly but gently in the direction of the hair growth all over him including down the legs and under the belly until you have covered the entire body by which time, if you have adopted a slow and steady rhythm, your horse will probably be almost asleep. If you are in doubt about the efficacy of hand grooming try it for a month and see the difference.

Ear Work

This is a targeted extension of hand grooming particularly designed to de-stress and calm the horse, but, some horses, for whatever reason, dislike their ears being touched. This is usually due to rough and inconsiderate handling in the past. Ear work must be carried out very gently and without pressure, do not try to force the issue as the ears are a very sensitive part of the horse.

Once you have accustomed your horse to having his ears touched we can tentatively begin work in earnest. When working the ears, start at the base of the ear, gently squeeze the two edges together and pull your hand along the length of the ear with a firm stroking action. The back of the ear should be in the palm of your hand and you should talk to the horse in a soothing voice at the same time. Repeat this process several times on each ear. If the horse likes it he will lower his head to you, if he doesn't you will soon find his ears out of reach. Next take the tip of the ear between your finger and thumb and rub gently, most horses really enjoy this as it is very relaxing and calming. I might add that this works on humans and dogs as well so you can try it on yourself.

Massage

The benefits of therapeutic massage have been known for thousands of years and nowadays massage is usually referred to as a complementary therapy. Whilst on people, it is frequently used as remedial action following injury or intensive exertion with horses its place is more properly before work to prepare the body for the job it has to do. Before you consider massage for your horse I should point out that under the Veterinary Surgeons Act of 1966 it is illegal for any person to practise massage on a horse (or any other animal) owned by another person without the consent of the veterinary surgeon who would normally attend that horse. What that means is that you can massage your horse yourself but you cannot pay a professional to do it without first asking your vet.

During massage we are working on the skin but it is frequently the underlying structures that are most affected. Massage affects two of the major systems of the body, the cardiovascular system or circulatory system and the lymphatic system. Very simply the cardiovascular system delivers oxygen and nutrients to the tissues via arteries and takes deoxygenated blood and waste products away via the veins. The lymphatic system is the 'drains' of the body for the collection of waste products particularly those produced by injury and illness.

Although we know massage to be generally beneficial there are a number of contra-indications. You should not massage if the horse demonstrates any of the following: is obviously sick; has any kind of skin condition; has 'tied up'; has any form of infection; is in-foal; has undiagnosed pain; is lame and has not been seen by a vet; has lymphangitis; has an abnormality that has not been diagnosed.

In addition do not massage over any kind of swelling; broken or inflamed skin; bony areas such as the ribs or the spinous process along the back; areas of soreness; any injury. You must also be aware that a good massage can radically alter the way a horse behaves from being an old plod to a sprightly spring chicken.

Different disciplines such as dressage and endurance require massage on different muscle groups but for the average horse owner the ability to deliver a basic relaxing massage for their horse will be sufficient.

Techniques

There are a number of different massage techniques ranging from the superficial to deep tissue involvement and unless you know what you are doing it would be wise to stick to the more superficial movements.

Effleurage

This technique is basically stroking and can be done one- or two-handed using the flat of the hand or the pads of the fingers if the areas in small and inaccessible. It is the initial movement that all good masseurs start with as it warms up the area of contact and prepares it for the deeper massage movements. It is probably the most useful massage technique for the average horse owner as it is, if done properly, deeply relaxing. Effleurage differs from hand grooming in that it is a two directional movement with an outward and return stroke. Pressure is exerted on either the outward or the return stroke by using the body weight to lean into it. Start with a light pressure and gradually increase this as the massage progresses and the horse relaxes. As a guide, your strokes should follow the direction of the main veins and if the horse were not covered in hair you would be able to see the skin becoming reddened with the increase in the blood supply. The main effects of effleurage are that it increases the blood supply to the skin, encourages the venous return and the flow of lymph and promotes relaxation. It also sooths tired, aching muscles.

Petrissage

Pertrissage is compression of the underlying soft tissue and although it is a one- or two-handed technique it is more usually performed using two hands. The underlying muscle tissue is picked between the ball of the thumb and the pads of the fingers into the palm of the hand, given a squeeze and allowed to relax back to the normal position. The hands are not taken away from the skin but work alternately with the accent on the picking up rather than the squeeze. On large areas of muscle as much of the hand as possible should be used with enough pressure to work the muscle but not so much as to cause pain. Repeat the movement a number of times over an area.

The benefits of petrissage are mobilization of tissue, reduction of muscle stiffness, relief of fatigue, reduction of tension under the surface of the skin, increase of nutrients to cells and mechanical relaxation.

Percussion

Also called tapotement there are a number of different hand positions that can be adopted for this movement but they are only suitable for use on large masses of muscle.

The actions should be performed with loose wrists so that one hand bounces off the muscle as the other strikes it. This can be done with either a loose fist in which case the muscle is struck with the outer edge of the hand or with the hands in a cup shape in when the muscle is struck with both edges of the hand.

Percussion sets up vibrations the effects of which are relaxing and rather like those of ultrasound. It also tones atrophied muscles if applied for short periods of time and stimulates nerve endings with a subsequent sedative effect if the movement is continued.

Friction

This technique is used one-handed and involves compression on a small area using the tip of the thumb or reinforced fingers. It can be superficial or very deep.

Friction is useful for working out knots in muscles. Working in very small circles the tips of the fingers do not move over the skin but do move the skin over the underlying tissue. At the same time pressure is exerted so that the whole movement is rather like spiralling downwards into the knot and then releasing. The movement is repeated several times on the same spot, each time increasing the pressure slightly. If you are lucky you will feel the knot release but care must be taken not to cause pain or damage tissue.

Friction generates heat and greatly increases the blood supply to the local area. Used properly it can free up restricted areas as it breaks down and separates adhered tissue. It is also known to increase the glandular action of the skin.

These are just a small selection of massage techniques that can be used and there are some excellent books on the subject of equine massage. If you are interested in giving your horse anything other than a very basic massage I would recommend training as, used incorrectly massage, has the potential to be very damaging.

Washing

Washing is certainly a lot easier than grooming to achieve the same effect but it should not be done too often as it will strip the natural oils from the coat and leave it dry and dull. Choose a very mild shampoo or one formulated especially for the purpose and check for any allergic reaction by doing a patch test, on an area where there is little hair, before washing the horse all over. Make sure you have enough warm water for rinsing as it is very important to get all the soap out of the coat. Washing your horse with cold water is as unpleasant for him as it would be for you and in winter is downright unkind, the water doesn't need to be hot just warm. Make sure you have plenty of clean rugs on hand as the last thing you want is for your horse to catch a chill.

The best way to wash your horse is to uses sponges and buckets. Start at the neck by wetting the coat and mane thoroughly, apply the shampoo to the sponge, this avoids any tendency to be over exuberant with the soap, and wash in a circular motion. Lastly wash the horse's face, taking great care not to get dirty water or soap in his eyes, and finally his tail. I personally leave this bit until after I have rinsed out the body and put a rug on but this is up to you.

Once you have washed the horse all over rinse with plenty of warm water until you have removed all the soap. Having made sure all the shampoo has gone from the coat remove any excess water with the sweat scraper followed by a brisk rub down with some clean towels which you can buy cheaply from charity shops. Lastly cover the horse with a clean rug to keep him warm and bandage his legs, you might also want to put on a tail bandage. One major point, it is important to dry the horse off as soon as possible after his bath, for this you might find an ordinary hair drier useful, paying particular attention to his heels.

Clipping

Shearing off your horse's winter coat is not something you should do lightly yet many people still do it unnecessarily every year. Your horse has grown this coat for a reason, namely to keep him warm and dry in inclement weather and here we are proposing to cut it all off to suit our own purposes. Clipping is interfering with nature so why do we do it? Each owner seems to have a different reason for clipping their horse ranging from making them look smart to ease of keeping them clean. There are of course perfectly valid reasons for clipping, the main one being to enable the horse to work comfortably in cold weather but we can't just clip without some prior thought and preparation. A horse that is clipped, unless it is a very low and narrow trace clip, will need to have his thermal insulation replaced by rugs and by stabling in winter. This adds up to a lot of time and work not to mention the expense of rugs and other equipment necessary for the stabled horse. If your horse does not go out in the field during the day he will need exercising for at least an hour to keep him fit and healthy and with mucking out, grooming and feeding you will need to have at least three hours a day to do your horse properly. The alternative is to keep him at livery but this can be very expensive. Other valid reasons for clipping include reducing sweating during work and preventing chills that may result from a heavy coat drying out slowly.

Having decided to clip your horse you will need a few basics.

- Two stable rugs
- Two turnout rugs
- Under rugs or blankets
- Anti sweat rug.

Note All horses and ponies that have any kind of clip will need to wear a turnout rug when out in the field.

If you decide to go for a full clip you will also need:

- Several sets of bandages and wadding
- Head and neck covers
- Exercise sheet.

As discussed earlier a horse grows two coats a year. Once clipped off the winter coat will not grow back, eventually it is replaced by the summer coat in the spring, although subsequent tidying up may be necessary several times in the interim. The best time to first clip a horse is when the winter coat is fully grown and set – sometime in October with subsequent clips as often as necessary after that. However beware of clipping too late in the season as this may spoil the horse's summer coat.

If you are going to pay somebody else to clip your horse do make sure they know what they are doing, until you experience it you have no idea how awful a bad clip looks. The key to a good clip if you are doing it yourself is to make sure your clipper blades are sharp. Experience will also help. When clipping do make sure you don't nick the skin and that the blades are cool.

You will also need to decide what type of clip you are going to give your horse. These are many and varied and people tend to make them up or kind of customize the old favourites, it will all depend on how much work your horse has to do. There are basically four types of clip of which all the others are a variation. These are the full clip, hunter clip, blanket clip and trace clip.

Full clip

In a full clip all the coat is removed, including the hair from the head and legs, with the exception of a small triangle at the root of the tail and a very thin strip at the roots of the mane. It is used on horses who are competing through the winter or who are in hard work. Before you start clipping make sure you have enough warm rugs and bandages.

Blanket clip

For a blanket clip the coat from the head, neck and belly is removed but the legs and a blanket shape from the withers over the loins is left on. A horse with a blanket clip will require rugging up the same as a horse with a full clip but will not require leg bandages.

Trace clip

This is a good clip for horses that work hard at the weekend but do very little through the week. It was originally used for harness horses that were clipped to the level of the traces. There are many variations of the trace clip, usually the underside of the neck and the belly are taken off but the head and the legs are left on. However in the chaser clip, a variation of the trace clip, the coat is taken off high up the neck and the head.

Hunter clip

In the hunting season, which is of course the winter, hunters work extremely hard. By the nature of the work they do their legs are vulnerable to thorns and knocks and the area under the saddle may become sore from being ridden all day. The coat from these areas is not removed in a hunter clip.

Types of clip

Hair has been removed from the shaded areas

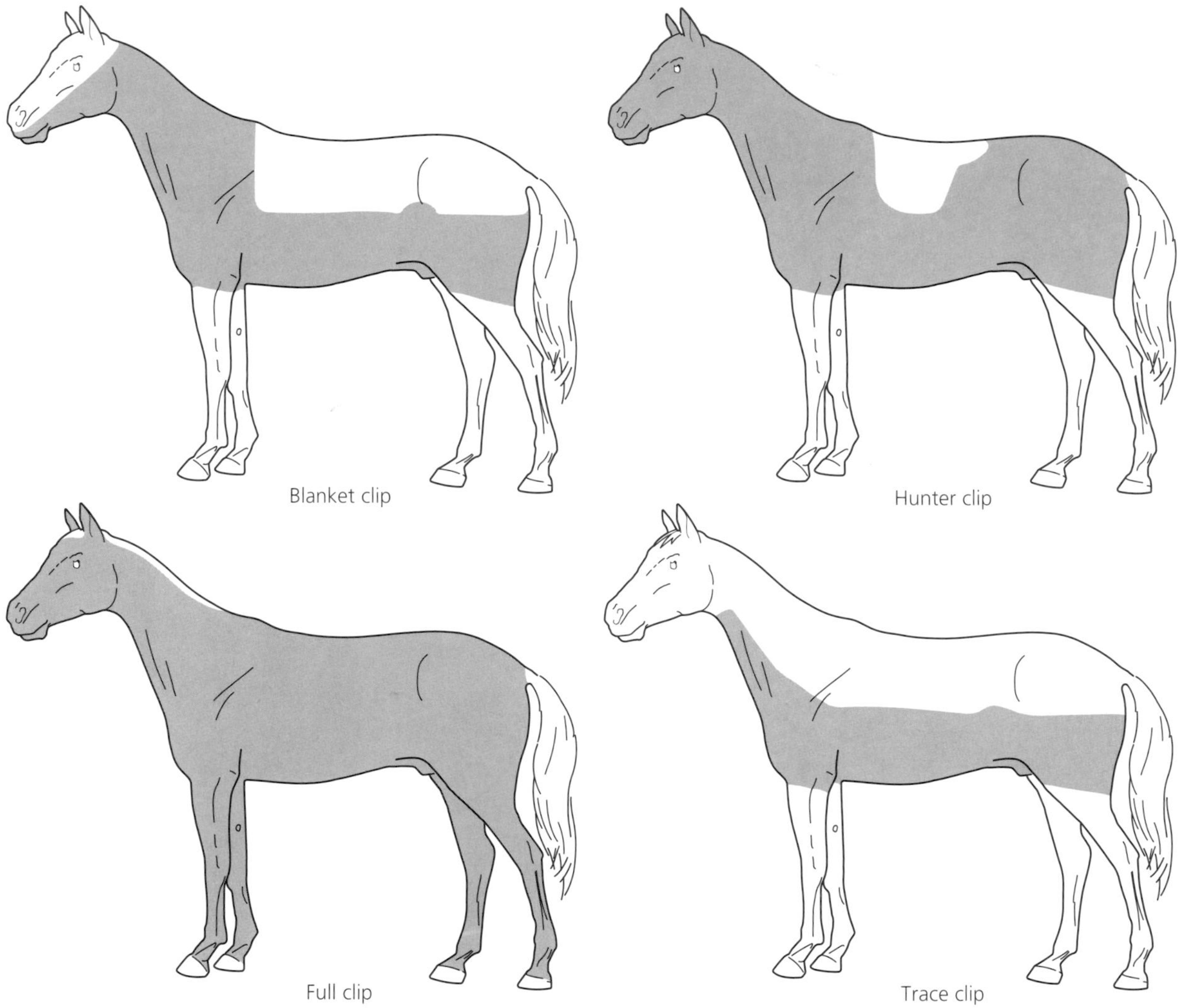

Blanket clip

Hunter clip

Full clip

Trace clip

Hogging

Hogging is when the entire mane and forelock is clipped off close to the neck. It is mainly used on cobs and polo ponies. Hogging can make a cob look extremely smart, polo ponies are hogged to prevent the rider's hands from becoming entangled in the mane, but whatever the reason for hogging is, the horse must have shelter away from the flies when out in the field. It goes without saying that once a horse is hogged you cannot plait his mane and will not

As a Shire cross cob, Polo's mane would be very coarse and thick and consequently difficult to manage. His appearance has been greatly improved by hogging.

be able to do so for at least six months. After a horse has been hogged, as the hair grows, it stands straight up from the neck like a brush so you will need to encourage it to lie over correctly.

Trimming

As with clipping we need to consider very carefully what we are doing when we trim. Trimming can vastly improve a horse's appearance but needless to say it comes with a price for the horse. The long hairs around the face and the feathers on the legs are there for a purpose. The hair under the jawline protects the head when grazing in very cold weather and the long hairs around the muzzle and the eyes act as feelers. There is some hair on the head that must not be trimmed on any account, this is the hair around the eyes and the hair inside the ears. The long hairs around the eyes protect them from damage whilst the hair in the ears stops the entry of insects and draughts. It is acceptable to trim round the ears to make them more shapely but do not remove the hair from inside them.

6.

Nutrition for a Healthy Skin

We are what we eat.

When I first started keeping horses the only compound feed that was available was pony nuts and everything else were what we call 'straights'. Straights are non-compounded feedstuffs such as oats, barley and maize a combination of which, mixed with bran and chaff, formed the basis of the concentrated feed for a horse. The principals of feeding a horse are much the same nowadays as they were then except that you don't have to mix the feed yourself, nowadays this is all done for you and proprietary food-stuffs can be bought by the bag for your convenience. Rightly or wrongly this means that there is no longer the need for horse owners to understand the ins and outs of feeding, it all comes ready formulated in a bag and all they need to do is to feed the correct amount.

There is a trend at the moment for feeding of supplements in the expecta-tion that this will correct any dietary deficiencies a horse may have. By and large, providing the horse is fed a suitable, balanced diet of roughage and con-centrates, supplements are unnecessary and therefore a waste of money but an inadequate or unbalanced feeding regime will very soon tell in your horse's skin and coat which will lose it's pliability and lustre.

There are some feedstuffs and additives that particularly affect the skin and coat and that, if included in the diet, will keep it supple and glowing with health, providing of course that the rest of the diet is up to scratch. You will find details of these further on in this chapter.

A Balanced Diet for Interior Well-Being

Before we consider what the balanced diet should consist of there are two cardinal rules to be followed when feeding horses.

1. Feed little and often. The smaller and more frequent the meals the better the horse will utilize his food.

2. Feed in line with the amount of work the horse is required to do.

A good basic diet includes protein, carbohydrates and fats in the right proportions along with vitamins, minerals and trace elements. There are two main reasons for malnutrition, one is that the horse is not getting enough calories and the other is malabsorption. As an added complication the owner may well be feeding the horse enough calories and there is nothing wrong with his digestion, but a very high parasitic burden, ether internal or external, is robbing him of his food.

Horses are sometime described as good or poor 'doers' and these are loose terms which refer to the amount a horse eats in relation to the condition he holds. A poor doer may need twice the intake of a good doer to maintain the same level of condition. The ability to 'do' well is influenced by the metabolic rate of the horse as well as a number of other factors and is frequently related to breed and disposition. A 'hot blooded' horse, such as a Thoroughbred, with a nervous disposition is likely to have a higher metabolic rate than a 'cold blooded' native pony such as a Dartmoor.

Skin problems connected to nutrition are very complex and can arise from many deficiencies, excesses and imbalances, however all of these produce only a limited set of skin reactions. The coat may become harsh, dry and brittle with large amounts of scurf and there may also be degrees of hair loss or alopecia. All of these signs could be the result of diseases other than poor nutrition and for this reason it is difficult to establish malnourishment as the cause of the condition by skin examination only.

At the end of the day, in horses, a deficiency or an excess of any of the essential nutritional requirements will lead to undesirable skin conditions.

Water

A horse can live for some time without food but only a few days without water, it is absolutely essential for life. Every horse, unless there is some very good reason, should have constant, unlimited access to fresh water and it should be clean. Water is vital. Lack of water or inadequate drinking leads to dehydration and dehydration leads to any number of ills. Apart from not drinking enough, dehydration can also result from loss of body fluid most commonly caused by severe diarrhoea or extended physical exertion in hot weather, but, deprivation of water for twenty-four hours will cause mild dehydration. Moderate to severe dehydration must be treated by a vet immediately, the loss of fifteen per cent of body weight in water can lead to the death of the horse.

Signs of dehydration are depression, weakness and lassitude, dry mouth and tongue, extended capillary refill time and sunken eyes. The extent of dehydration can be estimated from the elasticity of the skin. The best place to carry this test is on the skin just above the elbow. Pull this up into a peak, release and observe the time it takes to spring back into place. On a horse which is not dehydrated the skin will return to its normal position at once and with mild dehydration there will not be a great deal of different other than to the trained eye which no doubt you will develop in time, however with medium to severe dehydration the length of time that the skin remains in a peak is very noticeable. This is called tenting.

The Effects of Deficiencies on the Skin and Coat

Protein

Protein is necessary for growth and repair and normal maintenance of the skin and coat of a horse take up between twenty-five per cent and thirty per cent of the daily requirement. Hair itself is composed of ninety-five per cent protein with a high level of amino acids containing sulphur. The dietary protein requirement for horses is thirteen per cent and deficiency can lead to a number of diseases and conditions.

In animals suffering a lack of protein, the coat will become dry, dull and brittle. It will also be thin and easier to pull out than normal will take on a faded 'washed out' appearance caused by pigmentary disturbances of the skin and coat. The normal growth pattern of the hair will also be upset and the coat may take longer than usual to grow or shed.

Thickening of the outer, horny layer (hyperkeratosis) and thinning of the skin may be evident. With severe protein deficiency, excessive fluid (oedema) collects in the skin tissue.

Copper

Copper is an essential component of a number of the body's oxidative enzymes such as ascorbic acid. It may be deficient due to a lack of available copper in the diet or because it is blocked by interference in the absorption processes by zinc and calcium. Affected horses may show fading of the coat (leukotrichia)

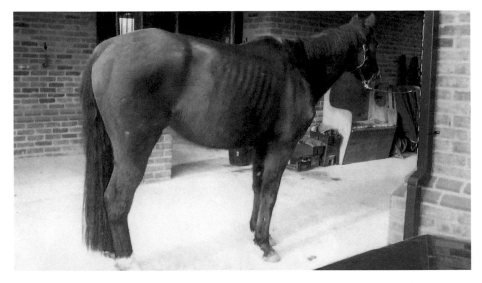

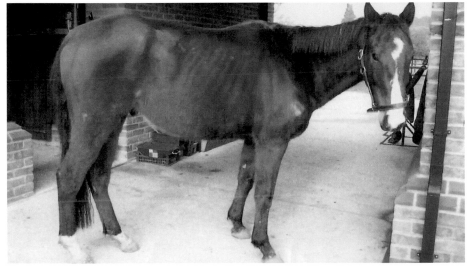

The effects of inappropriate management coupled with insufficient calorific intake have caused this horse to reach the point of emaciation. Although stabled at night with hard feed evening and morning, this Thoroughbred horse could not compete with more aggressive field companions for hay when out during the day. Not used to having to fight for his ration of hay his decline followed the introduction of a new pony. Unfortunately the stable owner failed to appreciate the problem or to notice that the horse had contracted ringworm. This can be seen as small, circular, bald patches on the hind leg and flank. There is also evidence of a rug rub on the point of the shoulder.

below The same horse, noticeably improved, ten days later. When this photograph was taken he was spending as much time outside as he had previously, and had a paddock to himself with other horses on the other side of the fence for company, consequently he was able to eat his own hay ration at leisure without interference. An improvement in the condition of his coat can also be seen.

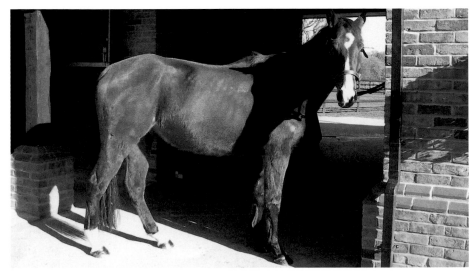

After eight weeks of proper management and an appropriate diet, not even the vet recognized this horse as being the one shown in the previous three photographs.

especially round the eyes giving them the appearance of wearing spectacles, they may also exhibit hair loss, stiffness and joint enlargement. Feed should contain at least 10md of copper per kg on the basis of ninety per cent dry matter. Copper deficiency is rare in adult horses and tends to occur in areas where copper is lacking in the grazing, in this country an occurrence of copper deficiency would be an unusual phenomena although it has been known in very copper deficient areas in the USA. Left uncorrected, animals deficient in copper will be unthrifty and, if young, slow to grow. Most properly balanced feeds will contain the correct amount of copper as will a good vitamin and mineral supplement. Where inhibition of uptake is suspected a vet should be consulted.

Iodine

Iodine is necessary for the functioning of the thyroid gland which amongst other things governs the metabolism. Mares that have been deficient in dietary iodine tend to have week foals that have varying degrees of hair loss and thickened, puffy skin. Lack of iodine in the diet is easily corrected by the provision of an iodised salt lick made freely available.

Zinc

Zinc is necessary for all sorts of bodily functions including skin growth and repair and wound healing, however naturally occurring, dietary deficiency in horses is so rare as to be almost unheard of. Experiments have been done on foals that were fed a diet with very little zinc in it. The foals developed skin lesions but happily these responded well once oral zinc was administered. The diet should contain at least 40mg of zinc per kg of dry matter.

Vitamin A

Vitamin A is fat soluble and can therefore be stored in the body. For this reason we not only have to make sure that the horse gets an adequate supply from his diet but that he does not end up with an excess. Many owners feed several supplements at once on the basis of a little being good so more must be better. This is not the case. With vitamin A both excess and deficiency produce the same results namely a rough, dull coat progressing to hair loss, scaling and thickening of the outer layers of skin.

Vitamin A deficiency also affects the hooves which may become dry and brittle and develop multiple vertical cracks with some horses developing inflammation of the coronary band (coronitis). Coronitis is characterized by flaking, exudation and subsequent crusting and sometimes by ulceration.

Of all the vitamins, horses are most likely to be deficient in vitamin A and this deficiency is found most frequently in young animals fed poor quality forage that has been stored for a long time. Vitamin A is almost never deficient in pasture-fed animals but where it is it is usually because the pasture is old and coarse. Of all the animals that are deficient the largest proportion are stable kept horses and it is worth noting that grains such as oats and barley are very low in vitamin A so if you are feeding straights make sure you feed high quality forage with them.

Feed Additions for Coat and Skin Improvement

Linseed

Linseed or flax seed is great for horses' coats and is an extremely good source of protein, however it must be thoroughly cooked first to get rid of the poisonous enzymes it contains, I find the best way to do this is for twenty-four hours in a slow cooker which I bought from a car boot sale especially for the purpose. The bottom oven of an Aga cooker will do just as well and you can of course boil it on an ordinary hob as long as you do it for long enough and have an extremely tolerant family who are prepared to put up with its rather earthy aroma. Properly prepared linseed will have the gelatinous consistency of frogspawn and should be cooked in small quantities and used fresh although it will keep for a couple of days in the fridge. If you feel like trying your hand at cooking for your horse do introduce it slowly, a couple of tablespoonfuls in his feed should be enough to start with, as for some horses linseed is an acquired taste. Once the horse has got used to it in his feed you can gradually increase the amount up to about 250ml (half a pint) once or twice a week.

Linseed should only be fed in small amounts as in large quantities it can act as a laxative however if you don't feel equal to cooking your own your feed merchant will more than likely carry a linseed oil feed additive.

Herbs

Herbs have been used for thousands of years for their medicinal properties but until recently they had become unfashionable in the face of modern pharmaceuticals most of which are, however, based on natural plant components. A proper mixed sward, that is the correct term for the plants growing in a pasture, consists of a mixture of different herbs and grasses growing in harmony, nowadays with the advent of more intensive farming the grass in your horse's field is more likely to consist of fast growing aggressive rye grass mixture or if the pasture has been badly managed or maintained, the more rank unpalatable grasses. Dried and crushed herbs can be added in small quantities to your horse's feed but this should be done with caution and under the guidance of a suitably qualified person.

Comfrey

Latin name *Symphytum officinale*, comfrey has long been used by horsemasters for therapeutic purposes. It is common in this country, growing wild in damp areas. The flowers can be blue or white and the leaves are tough and hairy.

Comfrey has excellent healing properties particularly for wounds, bruises, swelling and over-taxed muscles and for centuries it has been known to speed up the repair of broken bones earning the plant the common name of knitbone. Added to feed its anti-inflammatory properties make it excellent for pulmonary problems such as Chronic Obstructive Pulmonary Disease (COPD) and arthritis, especially in old horses.

Homoeopathic remedies are prepared from the fresh plant and apart from its bone healing properties the root of the comfrey plant produces a substance that promotes the growth of epithelium thus stimulating the healing of skin wounds and ulcerations. In the past many stables grew a patch of comfrey, the leaves of which could be applied fresh as a poultice or dried and crushed and added to the feed.

To make a comfrey poultice, boil the leaves and leave to cool. Apply the cooled leaves to the area to be poulticed and secure with a dressing or bandage. The poultice should not be left on for more than eight hours.

Fed in excess, comfrey can be toxic as it contains the same alkaloids as ragwort and for this reason it is not wise to feed it to regularly or for long periods of time. The alkaloids in question tend to be concentrated in the root so it is best to avoid this part of the plant. A small handful of dried or crushed leaves (20 to 30g) a day added to the feed would be an adequate amount.

Fenugreek

Latin name *Trigonella foenum-graecum*. This is another useful therapeutic herb that can relieve skin irritations and soreness.

Corn Oil

A proper balanced diet will naturally produce a glowing healthy coat but if you want to impart an extra special shine feed your horse corn oil in his daily ration. This can be given freely providing your horse will eat it but it must be gradually introduced. Up to 250ml can be given at one time but remember oils are rich in energy. Whilst fish oils such as cod liver oil will impart condition to the coat I would not advocate giving any animal or fish derivatives to a horse who is naturally vegetarian.

The use of corn oil was recommended to me by my vet who, at the time, was treating a mare with a serious liver problem. The mare made a full recovery and regained the healthy vibrant chestnut colour to her coat that had previously been a dusty, pale sandy colour.

7.

Protective Equipment – Horse Clothing and Tack

Materials for Clothing and Tack

Natural Materials

For use in horse clothing natural materials have advantages and disadvantages. Apart from leather, which is in fact cured skin, they are breathable and permeable making them more comfortable for the horse to wear and without doubt better for his skin. The disadvantages are that compared to synthetics, natural fabrics are heavier to wear and absorb moisture. They take longer to dry out if they become wet and they are less resistant to rips and tears. Compared to synthetics items made of natural materials are more expensive.

Leather

Leather is the traditional material used for saddles and bridles and has been in use for hundreds of years. The finest leather tack can be very expensive indeed but there are plenty of good quality mid range items that are perfectly serviceable and won't break the bank. Very cheap leather goods, usually from India and Pakistan, can be a total waste of money; at best they will not last the length of time good English leather will and at worst can be downright dangerous. It is no fun when your rein or your stirrup leather breaks when you're out riding. However in recent years some good cheap imported leather tack has come onto the market and very good value it is too. Whilst not suitable for the show ring it is perfectly adequate for everyday use. I myself have a smashing set of imported working harness which, whilst not particularly smart, does the job very well for schooling the pony and driving round the local roads.

Apart from buying an established make, good quality leather tack can be identified by its smell and general finish. Some Indian leather goods were made from uncured hides that had no smell at all, good leather smells wonderful. Needless to say the leather didn't last and was prone to tearing. I remember going into a saddlers as he was dismembering a very cheap Indian pony saddle only to find the tree was made of flattened baked bean cans! So if you choose leather find a reputable saddler, buy the best you can afford and look after it well.

Cotton

Used to make summer sheets that are lightweight and comfortable for the horse to wear and leg bandages. Cotton is a good lining fabric for rugs as it is absorbent and permeable. It lasts well provided it is kept clean and repaired.

Wool

Wool is undoubtedly warmer for the horse than many of the synthetic fabrics used to make horse clothing. Some horses are however sensitive to it and find it itchy next to the skin. It is used to make or line rugs and bandages.

Synthetic Materials

Synthetic materials are used nowadays for making a wide range of equine equipment from boots to saddles and they all have both advantages and disadvantages. On the plus side synthetics have more flexibility of use than natural fibres and are usually lighter to handle and for the horse to wear. They are also cheaper than natural materials.

Rugs made of synthetic materials can sometimes be washed and dried at home and they generally dry much quicker than those made of natural fibres. Similar advantages are to be found in synthetic saddles that will take a fraction of the time that leather takes to dry out after a good soaking. On the downside synthetic materials are usually non-absorbent and some are non-permeable. This makes them unhealthy for the horse's skin, non-permeable rug materials can lead to the horse becoming too hot under his rug and sweating. Sweat and moisture trapped next to the skin in a nice warm environment provides the ideal conditions for the proliferation of the micro-organisms responsible for causing skin disease.

Nylon webbing

Nylon webbing is used very successfully to make a range of bits of tack and equipment and it is extremely durable and strong. Nearly everybody is

The Pennine Senior stable rug. This rug was specially designed for the older horse. When a horse ages the withers and hip bones frequently have a tendency to protrude, providing a focus point for abrasion, and although highly absorbent, cotton can sometimes rub these sensitive areas. To prevent this the manufacturers have lined the Senior version of this range with nylon which is both lighter and less liable to cause rubs.

familiar with the ubiquitous nylon headcollars that are now extensively used but the range of goods made from nylon webbing is steadily growing and improving. Endurance riders favour bridles made of webbing but this trend has not yet caught on amongst other horse owners. Webbing bridles are extremely good value for money and compared to leather are relatively low maintenance. For the comfort of the horse they must be kept in good condition by regular cleaning as recommended by the manufacturer. Unfortunately they are still considered by the riding world to be somehow inferior. Another popular use for nylon webbing is competitive driving where whole sets of harness are made from it and compared to leather it is extremely lightweight.

Choosing Clothing and Tack

The keys to choosing horse clothing and tack are:

- Has it been designed for the job I want it to do?

- Does it fit my horse properly?

- Can I afford it?

- Do I really need it?

A 'no' answer to any one of these questions should lead to rejection of the item in question. Of the four the first two questions are all important and it is difficult to say which one of them is the most important, if it doesn't fit you shouldn't buy it but, regardless of fit, it is no use using a stable rug for turnout!

When buying secondhand tack and equipment we can add a fifth question. Is the condition serviceable? Yes to all the above – buy the kit.

Effects of Badly Fitting Tack

The effects of badly fitting tack are truly horrible and totally unnecessary. They fall into the category of trauma when we consider conditions that affect the skin. Horses that have white patches along the midline of the back or in the girth area have probably been subjected to trauma resulting in saddle sores or girth galls. This used to be a great deal more common than it is today.

A badly fitting saddle can have a profound effect on the horse. In the beginning he may put up with the discomfort but over time the discomfort increases and may develop into pain. At this point your horse will decide it is about time he did something about it. Probably his first tactic will be to try and avoid the pain by dropping his back and as a consequence raising his head, it will be more difficult for the rider to get the horse to work in an outline and when he does he will not sustain it. If the situation is allowed to continue the horse will become more and more stiff and resistive when working and then, out come the heavy duty training aids. The rider now tries to 'persuade' the horse, usually by gadgets and force to lower his head and work in a more rounded outline. All this makes the situation worse.

Having been thwarted in his first attempt at solving his saddle problem the horse starts to move in an unnatural manner as a means of pain evasion. The consequences of this are extra and unusual stresses placed on his joints, muscles, tendons and ligaments not to mention the continued trauma to the horse's skin. However things don't stop there. Due to the uneven movement the horse may start to wear his shoes unevenly and may be intermittently lame. Where the saddle tree is too narrow pressure can inhibit the circulation causing an inadequate supply of oxygen and nutrients and allowing the build up of waste products in the tissue. Deprived of oxygen the tissue will start to atrophy and become wasted with the horse developing hollows under the points of pressure. Necrosis of the skin and tissues caused by pressure on the spine leads to a most unpleasant condition called sitfasts. Sitfasts are the equivalent to corns in the back and we all know how painful corns can be, they are

The effects of badly fitting tack can be seen on the back of this horse. White patches of this kind are indicative of the horse having suffered from saddle sores that must have been extremely painful at the time. These injuries did not necessarily all happen at the same time, it is possible, if not likely, that this horse suffered from pain in the saddle area for a long time. The damage is superimposed on a previously inflicted freeze brand.

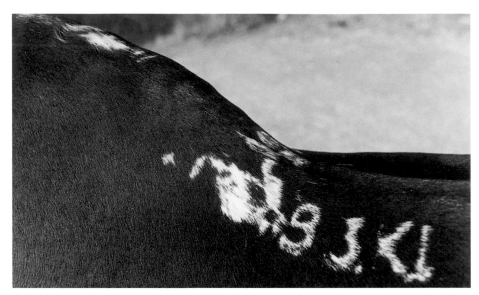

The same horse viewed from the right hand side showing more damage.

A wider view of the same horse's back. This horse has suffered considerable abuse in the past, apart from the damage to the withers and the back from badly fitting tack, the vertebra behind the saddle area are fused. The pain must have been extreme and prolonged.

extremely difficult to get rid of so it is better all round to prevent them from developing. Because of pain causing an inability to move freely and naturally the horse will begin to develop the wrong muscles which in turn alters the topline we all strive so hard to maintain.

To recap, from lack of attention to proper saddle fitting we have managed to achieve the following.

- A difficult horse that will not work in an outline.

- Is intermittently lame for no apparent reason.

- Has a ewe neck with a poorly developed topline.

- Doesn't relax or lie down.

- Is bad tempered when tacked up.

Finally, if your horse is showing signs of having a cold back do take it seriously and get the fit of your saddle checked.

It may come as a surprise but a badly fitting rug can do as much damage as a badly fitting saddle. It frequently escapes our attention that over the winter period some horses spend all day every day, with the exception of when they are ridden, in their rugs. This is currently compounded by the fashion for leaving a horse in his outdoor rug overnight in the stable instead of having a different 'night' rug to wear whilst indoors. A horse's skin is usually protected by a fairly thick layer of hair so you can imagine the friction which has to be exerted in order to render that skin as bald as can frequently be seen on the point of the shoulder in rugged horses!

Fitting

There is absolutely no way this book can turn you into an expert in fitting tack, particularly saddles, but what I am aiming to do is to give you a reasonable understanding of the subject so that you can feel easy that your horse is comfortable and his skin, which is what, in this book, we are all about, is not going to be damaged.

Badly fitting, uncomfortable tack or equipment can mean the difference between a well-behaved horse and a very, very badly behaved, fractious one but just because your horse doesn't behave badly doesn't mean his tack is comfortable or a good fit! Many horses are long suffering souls who are eager to please right down to not complaining about ill-fitting, uncomfortable tack. In the case of rugs a poor fit can affect your horse's action permanently. Too tight across his shoulders and he may alter his stride to accommodate the pressure from the rug, and, leave that rug on too long and his stride may be shortened permanently, catastrophic in a show or dressage horse. When buying a rug for your horse make sure you can return it if it is not a good fit, however it will not be appreciated or accepted if it is covered in horse hair. To avoid this try the rug on your horse over a thin clean sheet.

As with people, horses are never a standard size or shape so with off the peg rugs it will always be the best in the circumstances. Different manufactures make rugs to different patterns so it is as well to find a rug that fits your horse and stick to that make in future.

With saddles the very best advice I can offer is to find a good saddler who will visit your horse to fit his saddle and to check that fit on a regular basis.

There are many things to take into consideration when fitting tack, especially the saddle and as I have just said it is worthwhile locating a reputable saddler to fit your saddle for you. This is not always possible; nevertheless you need to do the best you can for both of you if you have to fit the saddle yourself.

If you have a young horse, in my opinion it is not worth spending a lot of money on a saddle as a horse's back can keep changing until they are about eight years old. This age is not set in stone as some horses mature quicker than others so you will need to exercise your judgment about it. As long as you check regularly that the saddle fits you will be fine. Also a horse's shape may be seasonally affected. Here, I am not talking about a horse that is underfed in winter but one who naturally carries more weight in the summer months. His basic shape will not change but a saddle that fits in July may not be such a good fit in February. Condition also plays a major part. There is a school of thought that the horse should muscle up to fit the saddle but an animal that is only ridden once or twice a week will not have the opportunity to do this.

When buying a saddle you will also need to consider the conformation of your horse and the job you want him to do. Usually a 'general purpose' saddle will do the job for you but occasionally the shape of the horse may dictate the type of saddle you buy. I have a cob that is so loaded on the shoulder that the saddle needs to be much more straight cut, rather like a show saddle.

One other thing I should mention, your horse must be 'comfortable' with the saddle. This sounds obvious but it is not to do with the fit, which may be fine, but is more to do with how your horse feels when you put the saddle on. Without doubt he will have a preference as to exactly where it is on his back but whether he will express that preference is another matter. Now, with most horses the indications of preference may be absent or infinitesimally small. Horses that have been passed round a number of owners have a tendency to internalize their problems and discomfits and become very adept at concealing them, however in some cases the horse will let you know that the saddle is not in what he considers to be the correct place. At this point I can hear you speculating that I am barking mad – not so – my cob, again, is almost unrideable if his saddle is not in exactly the right place. He is of course an extreme example but this self-expression on his part is likely to save him from back injuries resulting from a badly fitted saddle, it is something we should be aware of.

Saddles

In order to be able to fit a saddle properly we must first understand the structures that it sits on. To be in the right place the saddle must sit in the lowest part of the horse's back. The spine, running down the centre of the back, is made up of bones called vertebrae. These have a hole through the middle of them through which runs the spinal cord. Vertebrae have long bony projections from the top called spinous process and from the side called transverse processes. The spinous and transverse processes are attachment points for muscles, ligaments and tendons and the transverse processes are also attachments for the ribs. In the horse the spinous process of the front thoracic vertebrae are angled back towards the tail, these gradually become more upright until they meet the lumbar vertebrae whose spinous process point in the opposite direction, in other words from tail to head. The anticlinal vertebrae actually has an upright spinous process, this area is the weakest part of the horse's back and is unfortunately where the rider sits. The spinal column, the eighteen thoracic vertebrae, the scapular or shoulder blade, the wither and the ribs form the main support for the saddle. Over these structures lie the back muscles which run down either side of the spinous process and are attached to the bones of the skeleton by tendons. A badly fitting saddle will affect three major muscles, the latissimus dorsi, logissimus dorsi and the trapezious but putting the saddle in the wrong place on the horse's back will also cause problems.

To locate the saddle in the correct place, start by placing it well forward over the withers. Slide the saddle back as far as it will go, it should now be sitting in the lowest point of the horse's back but this will depend on the conformation of the horse. The points of the saddle tree should sit comfortably in the hollows behind the shoulder blades, any further forward and the saddle will impede the movement of the horse's shoulder and may cause saddle sores. A saddle that is fitted too far back will very rapidly cause bruising and make the loins sore.

Off the peg and secondhand saddles are found in three general widths, narrow, medium and wide although it is possible to find extra wide fittings. A saddle that is the wrong width for your horse will cause serious back problems. One that is too narrow will also be too high at the pommel. The effect of too narrow a saddle is to cause excessive pressure on either side of the back under the points of the tree. This bruises the muscles and produces pain and sores. A saddle with a gullet that is too narrow will pinch the back on either side and

A good saddle position

A badly fitting saddle can affect these muscle groups.

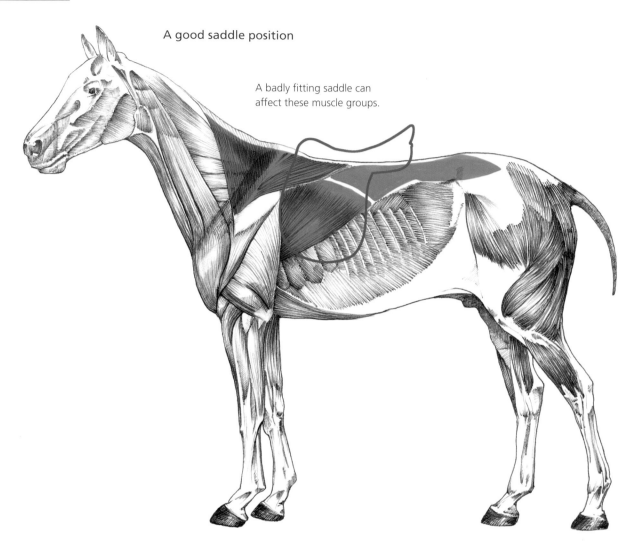

is likely to affect the paces which may become uneven. Lateral flexibility will be lost and the back will stiffen up and continuous use without correction will result in pain. A well made saddle should have a gullet with a width of at least three fingers so that it can rest comfortably on either side of the spinal column with the rider's weight distributed evenly over the full bearing area and with sufficient clearance of the spine.

A saddle that is too wide will not have enough clearance over the withers and will be too low on the horse's back. This will cause the sensitive wither area to become traumatized leading to pain and saddle sores.

To check the fit of a saddle stand the horse on even, level ground and check that his back is clean and he has no sore areas including around the girth. Do not try to fit a saddle on a horse that is lame or who has a known back problem. Locate the saddle in the right place on the horse's back and fasten the girth. As you are doing this look out for signs of discomfort or irritation by the horse such as flattening the ears, fidgeting and moving around or nipping. Assuming that there are none check the following points:

- The points of the saddle tree should be at least two finger widths clear of the shoulder blades on either side.

- The pommel must be well clear of the withers. Check this with your hand to make sure that the saddle cannot rub or put pressure on any part of the wither, you also need to check this with a rider on board.

- The panels should fit closely against the horse's back with contact all along the length and must be clear of the spine.

- The seat of the saddle should be level and should feel level and comfortable when you are riding in it.

- When riding does the horse move freely and feel relaxed?

- Unsaddle the horse and check the panels for areas that did not come into contact with the back. Unless your horse is exceptionally clean these will appear as patches without dirt on them. Run your hand over the back and withers where the saddle has been and look for any areas of sensitivity.

Once you have found a saddle that fits your horse it will need to be maintained in good condition by regular cleaning and remember the horse's back changes from time to time so you need to check the fit on a regular basis.

Bridles

There are numerous different types of headgear which we collectively call bridles and these can be with bit or without it. The key is that the horse must be comfortable with what he is wearing and this includes whatever, if anything, is in his mouth.

It is of little use if the bridle fits perfectly but the bit pinches the lips or if the bit is exactly the right size but the headpiece is rubbing behind the horse's ears. A simple bridle consists of a browband, a headpiece, two cheek pieces, a pair of reins and maybe, a noseband of one sort or another. The browband should be long enough to reach across the forehead from the headpiece located behind the ears on either side, without sagging at the front or pulling the headpiece forward and interfering with the ears. The headpiece itself should be large enough to allow for plenty of adjustment for the cheek pieces but not so long that the cheek pieces have to be set on the last hole for the bit to hang in the correct place in the mouth. In addition the throatlash part of the headpiece should allow for at least three fingers of room when done up. Too tight and the horse will be in discomfortt from pressure on the throat, too loose and you may

This horse is wearing a corrcetly-fitted international flash bridle.

below A correctly-fitted competition flash bridle.

lose the bridle altogether. Cheek pieces attach the bit to the headpiece and should be long enough to allow for the correct fitting of the bit, whatever bit you choose. The bit itself must not hang too low in the mouth and bang on the teeth, neither should it crease the corners of the mouth beyond a slight upward wrinkle. The most basic bridle consists of all the above plus a set of reins. The length of rein will depend on the length of neck of the horse but they should allow the horse to stretch his neck out without pulling the rider's hands forward yet not be too long that they become trapped by the saddle.

To the above most people add a noseband and there are a variety of these to choose from, all serving a different purpose. The basic straightforward cavesson does little more than provide decoration for the horse's face and when fitted correctly should allow for two fingers between the band and the skin. Regrettably over the past few years a deplorable fashion has sprung up for cranking the nosepiece so tight to the extent that you cannot get even one finger between the band and the horse's face with the consequence that the horse cannot move his jaw. This, in my opinion, is unkind and grossly unfair to the horse and anybody who does it on my horses is told not to in no uncertain terms. There are two other types of noseband in common use and these are the drop noseband and the flash. It is most important that these are fitted correctly as both can potentially interfere with the horse's breathing. However we are not about fitting and the use of the more specialist bits of kit but about its affect on the horse's skin if it is a) the wrong size, b) is in poor condition and causes chafing and c) is fitted too tightly with the same effect.

Snaffle bridle with cavesson noseband correctly fitted.

Headcollars

Having talked about bridles we must now consider headcollars. These are a prime source of abrasions to the head and unless your horse is very difficult to catch it is better not to leave his headcollar on in the field. Headcollars that are too tight, presumably to stop them coming off, have a habit of rubbing under the jawbone and can cause open sores that will inevitably attract flies in the summer months. The finest headcollars are made of leather but nowadays people usually keep these for best and use the perfectly serviceable nylon variety for everyday use.

A correctly-fitted headcollar – the cheek piece.

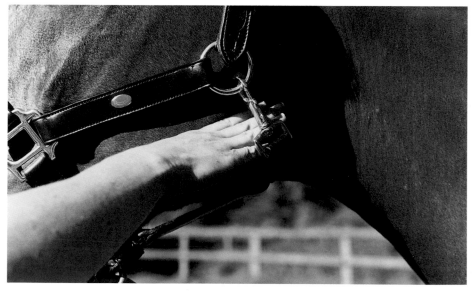

A correctly-fitted headcollar – the throat piece.

A correctly-fitted headcollar – the noseband.

A correctly-fitted headcollar.

Rugs

Years ago rugs used to be held in place by a tight band round the horse's middle called a surcingle or, if it was an up-market yard, an anticast roller. Horses were 'girthed up' at night to hold the rugs, usually made of jute, in place, which must have been jolly uncomfortable for the horse. Under the jute rug were blankets, quite often made of itchy wool and on top of the jute rug, under the surcingle discerning owners placed a foam or sheepskin pad in the hope of preventing a sore back or sitfasts. All this lot took a fair bit of skill to arrange and resulted in a certain amount of pride when, in the morning, it was found to be still in place and not hanging between the horse's front legs or trampled into the bedding! It also caused a lot of bad backs in horses. Fortunately, times have changed. Nowadays rugs have cross surcingles that are attached and are much more loosely fitted, rollers are generally confined to use when lungeing.

I will not bore you with a description of fitting the old-fashioned type of rugs as it is quite enough to fit a modern one properly. Fitting from the front to the back the rug must lie comfortably above the withers. The neck should not be so loose at to allow the rug to slip back behind the withers or drop down below the point of the shoulders. A stable rug should extend all the way back to the root of the tail with a turnout rug being slightly longer. Rugs tend to vary in depth but must come at least to below the elbow and stifle. Extra deep rugs are now available which minimize draughts around the belly. Once the rug is on the horse there should be no creases or obvious stretch/pull points and he must be able to get his head down to eat and move about without causing him any discomfort. Turnout rugs should be a little more generous in their fit.

If the rug has cross surcingles there should be at least a hand's breadth of room between the strap and the horse's belly and the same with the leg straps. Above all a rug should offer no restriction in movement or pose any risk of injury.

There are many different designs of rug and it goes without saying that a rug that is tailor made for your horse will always fit better than an off the shelf one,

This horse is wearing an old fashioned jute rug, held in place by a surcingle round the belly. This type of clothing has now largely been superseded by the more modern type of rug with attached surcingles that puts less pressure on the spine. Incorrectly fitted surcingles, used in ignorance without a back pad were responsible for sitfasts in many horses.

these however tend to be expensive. One other point to mention, if your horse has a bad or injured/sore back try to avoid rugs that have a seam down the middle. The ill effects of a rug that does not fit very well can be partially relieved by a bib which is worn under the rugs and covers the chest and shoulders.

The Odd-Shaped Horse

Most horses are more or less symmetrical but occasionally you will come across a horse that is a different shape on one side from the other. This type of horse needs to be very carefully fitted for tack and rugs or there is likely to be trouble ahead. The odd shape could be a result of injury or deformity but whatever the cause you cannot put standard tack on him and expect to get away with it.

Rugs, Blankets, Bibs and Hoods

There is a vast array of horse clothing to choose from, from the very basic to the extremely fancy. Rugs, blankets, bibs and hoods are there to protect the skin and keep the horse warm and dry in inclement weather. Rugs are categorized by the job they are intended for which will also dictate what they are made of. A clipped and stabled horse will need at least two types of rug and should have at least two of each type. This is to allow for one being cleaned

A correctly-fitted stable rug. The design of this rug features detachable cross surcingles and double breast straps. It has one hundred per cent heavy duty cotton lining with 4oz hard-wearing nylon outer. D rings facilitate the attachment of a neck cover. These rugs can be bought in a range of different weights.

A correctly-fitted turnout rug. This one has a wrap-around fit, action gussets for ease of movement and soft wither and shoulder pads. This rug is made from 12oz ripstop poly/cotton with a 170g loose-quilted lining encased in one hundred per cent heavy duty cotton drill.

while the other is in use. In addition to all the different types of rug there is also a range of different weights and warmth factors. The type of rug you need, will depend on the type of horse you have and what you want to do with him.

A horse or pony's ancestry dictates the density of the winter coat he grows and this in turn will dictate the selection of rugs. A Thoroughbred or Arab, whose coat is not designed for our so called temperate climate will need a rug in winter even if he is not clipped out where as a native pony is more than adequately insulated against our coldest winter.

Stable/Night Rugs

This type of rug is non waterproof so is not for outside use and as its name implies it is for use in the stable. The name night rug comes from a time when horses were more commonly kept stabled unless they were out exercising, and by that I don't mean grazing in the field. In those days a horse wore a different set of rugs during the day that were called, yes you've guessed it, day rugs.

Once again it is a case of making sure the rug fits the horse properly so that there is plenty of room for his shoulders to move and that it does not rub him at the front. Breathable material is best so that moisture can travel away from the skin. If the weather becomes very cold two rugs can be used together or you can buy an under rug. Fleeces are extremely useful both as under rugs and on their own if a horse is stabled but not clipped. One word of caution, wool next

The winter coat of a native cross pony. As you can see there is a good long, thick covering of hair to keep him warm. In a pure native pony the coat would be denser still, whilst a Thoroughbred would have considerably less.

to the skin can cause irritation in horses the same way as it does to some people so if you find your him scratching, investigate.

Turnout/New Zealand

New Zealand rugs are traditionally made of waterproofed canvas with a blanket lining, they have no surcingles but they do have leg-straps. New Zealand rugs do not have much shape to them and rarely have tail flaps, they also have a tendency to become waterlogged in very wet weather and take an age to dry out. Nowadays they have largely been replaced by rugs made of synthetic fabrics that resist extreme weather better, dry out more quickly and are lighter weight for the horse to wear.

Hoods and Neck Covers

Hoods and neck covers can be worn inside in the stable and outside in the field and are made in a range of appropriate materials. Elasticated hoods are very good for keeping the head and neck clean and laying the mane flat. Both stable and turnout rugs frequently come with the option to buy hoods and neck covers that match them and can be attached with clips and hooks. Some rugs can be bought that have integral neck covers.

Exercise Sheets

Exercise sheets are usually waterproof with an absorbent lining, although they can be made of wool or synthetic material. They are worn by clipped or sensitive horses when out at ridden exercise to protect the loins and the rump and are fitted under the saddle. They are very useful for keeping a clipped horse warm and dry in wet and windy weather without.

Summer Sheets

Summer sheets are usually made of cotton and are worn in the summer whilst travelling or in the stable. Their primary use is protection to keep dust off the coat and not to provide any warmth but they also have a role in protecting the horse from flies.

Mesh Fly Rugs

Fly protection of this kind is directly defending the skin against attack. During the summer months horses are tormented by flies to a greater or lesser degree depending on where they are kept and the amount of shelter there is. Some horses react very badly to being bitten by flies whilst others seem to handle it without too much trouble. For the sensitive equine mesh rugs can be a god-send allowing them some measure of peace when out in the field but they do have their down sides and I have to say as yet I am in two minds about them. The problem is that some flies have a tendency to get trapped underneath the net which, being unable to dislodge them, must be torture for the horse. However, the design of this protection against flies is constantly improving, and the makers may now have solved that problem. Combined with a fly screen or hood it is now possible to cover the entire horse, with the exception of the legs, with mesh.

Fly Screens and Fringes

There are several different types of both screens and fringes and both are made with and without 'ears'. The mesh fly screens that cover the front of the face rather like a visor on a helmet are splendid for keeping flies out of the horse's eyes and ears if it is an eared variety. However I would not recommend the use of some fly fringes as it is my observation that the longer kind can spread diseases such as conjunctivitis from one eye to the other.

Bibs

Bibs are worn primarily to help prevent chaffing on the chest from not so well fitting rugs. There are a number of different designs from the shaped and quilted tube to the fancy contraptions that fasten between the horse's front legs and round the barrel behind the elbows. I have found that some types do

above left Full face mask. Comfortably fits from tips of ears to the end of the muzzle. Provides excellent protection from flies, midges and sunburn. Adjustable and detachable nosepiece allows you to tailor the fit to each horse or to remove completely (*above right*).

Fly mask. Fits very comfortably over the horse's head, providing excellent clearance for eyes and eyelashes. Soft padding at the brow and noseband prevents rubbing. Adjustable fastenings under the cheeks and behind the ears ensure the perfect fit.

above left Muzzle net for head shakers. A shaped mesh that fits neatly over the horse's muzzle and attaches to the bridle via a padded noseband. Improves seventy-nine per cent of sufferers in clinical trials. Permitted by the British Dressage and British Eventing.

above right Fly mask for ridden work. The mask attaches easily and neatly to the bridle, and does not have to be removed when taking off or putting on the bridle. It offers clarity of vision for the horse so the rider can be confident that the horse can see clearly.

the job better than others, the best one to date having been bought in America. This one is made of anti-sweat mesh lined with a soft synthetic material and with Velcro fastenings to stop it slipping forward and rucking. Bibs can be bought made of all sorts of material both natural and synthetic but whatever they are made of they should be soft on the skin.

Numnahs

Numnahs are made of all sorts of different materials some of which are good for the skin and some not so good. Unfortunately numnahs don't always protect the horse's back in the way we think they might. If your saddle fits your horse properly don't use a numnah as it will interfere with the fit of the saddle. Imagine having a pair of comfortable shoes and then wearing them with several pairs of thick socks, this would make them a very tight fit. Putting a numnah under a saddle that fits properly will have the same effect, making it tight on the back and possibly leading to pinching and bruising.

Numnahs do however have a place and are very useful when a saddle is a little too wide and does not quite fit as well as it might. The best sort are made of absorbent material.

Boots, Bandages and Accessories

Boots

There is an enormous range of boots available for horses for all sorts of different disciplines and all of them are aimed at protection of the skin and the underlying structures. Once a joint or tendon is damaged by bruising or being struck into by an opposing leg, recovery can be quite protracted and if it continues to happen will lead eventually to enlargement of the joint. Choosing the right boot for the job can be a minefield for the uninitiated not to mention fitting them properly.

Equine Chaps for Turn-Out

These help keep horse's legs clean, warm and mud free. The chaps encase the horse's lower leg in breathable Stomatex, fitting over the hoof and under the heel. They come in varying sizes

If you think your horse is likely to strike himself during work do take the trouble to use boots. These must be clean especially on the inside otherwise dirt and grit will abrade the skin negating any value you may gain by using the boots. One other word of warning, if you are working your horse in a sand-

Equine chaps for field wear.

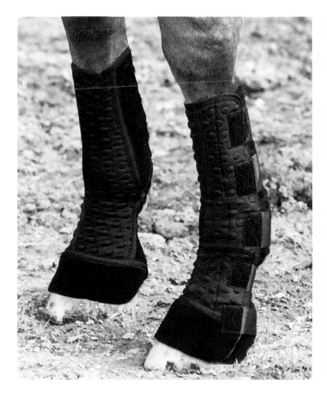

school use padding and bandages instead of boots. It is all too easy for sand to get between the boot and the skin and cause rubs.

Brushing boots

I should think that almost all horse owners have a set of these boots if no others. They are the most common boot in use and in some case are used incorrectly when another boot may be more appropriate. They are designed to protect the lower part of the leg from banging or brushing against the opposite leg during work. Brushing boots have a reinforced area that runs from the fetlock up the inside of the leg, speedicut boots which are a type of brushing boot, are slightly longer and provide protection further up the leg from just under the knee, in front, and the hock behind.

Brushing boots are fastened with either buckles or Velcro on the outside of the leg, they should not be so loose that they slip down nor so tight as to interfere with the tendons.

Fetlock or anti-brushing ring

This is only fitted to the leg that needs protection and acts as a buffer round the fetlock to fend off any interference. It does not provide as much protection as a Yorkshire boot and some horses actively dislike it as it upsets their natural action. The sausage boot is a thicker version and is meant to protect the elbows when the horse lies down.

right Brushing boots. These protect the legs from knocking against each other, causing trauma and injury

far right Anti-brushing ring.

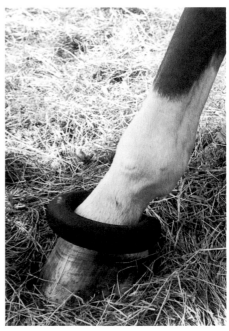

Fetlock boots

Also called ankle boots these are like a shortened version of brushing boots. Some designs come round underneath the fetlock at the back and protect the ergot growing down from the point of the fetlock. Yorkshire boots which consist of thickish woollen material fastened with tape and folded over are a very simple type of fetlock boot. These boots are perfectly adequate when the level of protection needed is only slight or when the horse goes just a little close behind.

Heel boots

Like the fetlock boots they also protect the ergot by passing under it. They are designed for use during fast work or jumping to protect the back of the foreleg from injury by the horse's hind feet, reinforcing is therefore down the back. It is also possible to get a combination of heel and brushing or speedicut boots.

Over-reach boots

Over-reach or bell boots protect the heels and coronets from damage caused by the hind hooves striking into them. They should always be worn when the horse is doing fast work, jumping or when the horse is being lunged. There are several different patterns of over-reach boot with different types of fastenings. These fastening can come undone so although they are inconvenient to put

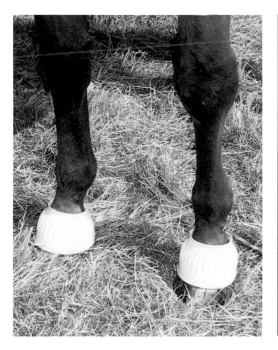
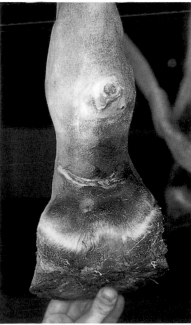

Over-reach boots to prevent the type of injury shown (*right*).

on and take off the best type of boot to use is the all-in-one rubber type that pull on over the hoof. Over-reach boots are usually only fitted at the front but may be used all round when travelling to protect from side-stepping. Fitting these boots properly is very important as they can themselves cause chaffing in the sensitive areas of pastern. Once on the horse they should not touch the ground at the back.

Tendon boots

Once again these are designed to protect the front legs from damage by the rear but what they do not do is support the tendons against strain. The reinforced protection is down the back of the leg and a combination tendon and brushing boot is also available with corresponding protection down the inside.

Travelling boots

There are lots of designs of these boots, both long and short, for use, as the name implies, when boxing your horse. Most of them incorporate protection for the knees and the hocks and they are basically thick, shaped pads with Velcro fastenings. Short travelling boots should be used in combination with knee and hock boots.

Knee boots

Knee boots protect the knees when travelling or doing roadwork. The type of knee boots used for travelling tend to be more substantial whilst those used for

right Tendon boots.

far right Travelling boots protect the horse's legs when being boxed.

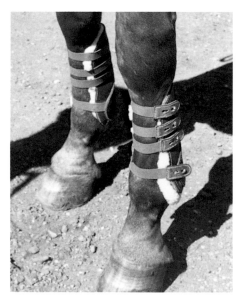

work have a reinforced pad covering the patella or knee cap with straps which fasten above and below the knee. The strap above the knee should be fastened quite snugly whilst the one below the knee is left quite loose.

Hock boots

Fitted in the same way as knee boots but for the hind legs with reinforcing to protect the point of the hock. These boots are designed for protection during travelling or in the stable. They should not be left on too long as they are enclosing a major joint. Whilst I'm sure hock boots have their place in the grand scheme of things, for travelling I prefer long travelling boots and in the stable, where a horse is likely to damage himself, extra bedding.

Bandages

There is a variety of bandages for different purposes and they are made in a variety of different materials and a range of colours, some of which are distinctly lurid.

Old-fashioned bandages were secured with tapes, knotted and tied in a bow before being tucked into the bandage on the outside of the leg. These had a nasty habit of coming undone at the worst possible moment; fortunately Velcro is now a more common mode of fastening.

Applying bandages correctly and safely is a bit of an art form but with practice it is a skill you can acquire relatively easily. For safety reasons there are a

below left Knee boots. These protect the knees when riding fast or on hard surfaces.

below right Hock boots. These boots are designed for protection of the hock when travelling or when in the stable. They should not be left on too long as they are enclosing a major joint.

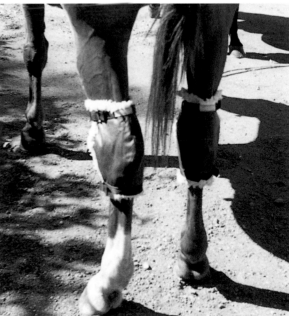

few very important rules about bandaging – the bandages should not be too loose, they should not be too tight and they should not come undone unless you undo them.

Exercise bandages

Exercise bandages were originally thought to provide support for the tendons but this is no longer held to be true, they do however give protection against knocks and bruising. This type of bandage is made of stretch material and care must therefore be taken not to put them on too tight. Exercise bandages should always be put on over some kind of padding. This is available in sheets specially made for the purpose and can be reused a number of times. The alternative padding still much favoured is gamgee tissue, a type of gauze and cotton wool sandwich. To provide enough padding two layers of gamgee are needed and great care must be taken to make sure it is flat and wrinkle free.

The correct application of exercise bandages is extremely important as put on badly, they have the potential to do significant damage. Too loose and they may come undone and trip the horse up, put on too tight they can restrict the circulation and produce pressure injuries and if they are uneven they can cause friction and, again, pressure.

Every horse owner needs to learn to bandage correctly and the only way to learn is to practise. To start with try it out on an inanimate object like a table leg before progressing to a quiet horse or pony.

Stretch and flex boots for flatwork. They are pliable and flexible allowing the horse to move freely, without any feeling of restriction. Made from breathable Stomatex, the boots help the horse's skin temperature to remain at a comfortable level.

Stable bandages

The primary function of stable bandages is to keep the horse's legs warm but they are frequently used to protect the legs when travelling and to exert a slight pressure on legs that are inclined to fill overnight. Another common use of stable bandages is to hold other bandages and dressings in place. Stable bandages are not stretchy and should be longer than exercise bandages although the cheaper makes are to my mind not long enough, the best are made of knitted wool or cotton but there are synthetic ones on the market. As with everything else you get what you pay for so it is worth while investing in a good set as they will undoubtedly last much longer than the cheaper varieties.

Tail bandages

Tail bandages are made of crêpe and are therefore stretchy. They are used to protect the tail and to keep it in a neat shape. As tail bandages are not used over padding care must be taken not to damage the fine skin under the tail or the dock or to put the bandage on too tightly.

Cohesive bandages

These stick firmly and securely to themselves and they are reusable a few times. Because they stick to themselves they are very useful for holding padding in place for exercise or dressing following injury but they should not be put on the legs without padding underneath. Cohesive bandages can also be used as tail bandages for veterinary procedures or at foaling time and there should be a good stock of them in the first aid kit.

Other Items of Tack and Equipment

Poll guard

This protects the sensitive area between the horse's ears on the top of the head and is an essential piece of kit that most people don't seem to own. Horses are extremely vulnerable in this spot and have been known to drop down dead after a bang on the head between the ears. Poll guards are mainly used when travelling but occasionally a horse that throws his head about or is known to rear will wear one in the stable.

Poll guards are made of either synthetic material or leather. They have holes for the horse's ears and slits for the headpiece of the headcollar to pass through. Basically it is a reinforced, padded cap that sits on the top of the head and is held in place by the headcollar. It goes without saying that it should be kept

A poll guard, a reinforced, padded cap that sits on the top of the head and is held in place by the headcollar.

clean but extra care must be taken to ensure that the edges of the ear holes do not rub the delicate skin round the ears.

Tail guards

Tail guards are used to protect the top of the tail from damage when travelling and are made of either leather or fabric. They fasten with either tapes or Velcro and have a tape that passes through a loop on the travelling rug to hold it in place. Tail bandages serve the same purpose but have the added advantage of holding the tail in a nice neat shape.

8.

Conditions and Diseases

Before we embark on the descriptions of the various skin diseases it would be as well to understand one or two things. For instance we need to know the difference between the signs of a disease and its symptoms. A sign of a disease is an indication or something that can be seen, it is objective and measurable. An example of a sign of skin disease would be dandruff, (or more correctly pityriasis), which is a clinical sign of a number of skin diseases.

A symptom is something a horse would complain of, if he could talk, so a good example of a symptom would be pain. The symptoms of a disease are subjective.

An injury under the jaw line caused this vein to protrude. The condition is irreversible.

When to Call the Vet

The 'watch' words here are 'don't take any risks' as time might be of the essence, it is unlikely with skin diseases but remember the skin problem might be a symptom of something else more insidious. If you are in any doubt or you notice any of the 'red flag' signs call the vet immediately even if it is out of normal working hours. Your vet will listen to your description of the symptoms your horse is exhibiting so it is a good idea to make a note of these first so that you don't leave any out. He will particularly want to know obvious things such as the horse standing up or are there any signs of pain or fever.

'Red Flag' Signs

'Red flags' are signs and symptoms that will alert you to the fact that something is seriously wrong and needing urgent veterinary intervention. If you notice any of them do not hesitate to consult your vet. The red flags are not peculiar to the skin but all of them will in some way be reflected in the condition and appearance of the skin. All red flag signs along with many others will predispose *stress*.

The things you should look for are:

- Pain that has not been diagnosed.

- Raised temperature – the temperature of an adult horse is between 100° to 101° F or 37° to 38° C. A rise in temperature is normal after exercise but a temperature of 102° could be serious.

- Laboured or difficulty in breathing.

- Inability to rise.

- Staggering.

- Unexplained sweating.

- Sensitivity to light.

- Unpleasant discharge.

- Loss of blood.

- Scouring (diarrhea).

- Absence of droppings.

- Extreme thirst.

- Dehydration.

- Lacklustre appearance and loss of appetite.

Conditions Which Predispose Disease

When we consider the sort of conditions that predispose stress in the horse something that is overlooked much of the time is the owner. Horses are sensitive creatures and if an owner is stressed for any reason, they will pick up on it. Your horse looks to you to provide him with all of his basic requirements including his security and if you yourself are agitated and upset it will inevitably upset him. You, therefore, owe it to yourself and your horse to look after yourself both mentally and physically. This is the beginning of providing your horse with a stress-free environment.

Stress

Stress can have a huge negative impact on health so a thorough assessment of the whole aspect of your horse's life and incidentally your own, is well worth the trouble. Start by having a good look at his environment. Does he have enough to eat and adequate shelter? Is he warm enough or is he too hot? Is he in any pain, do his teeth need attention? Once you have identified and corrected any stressful circumstances and satisfied yourself that all is well on these scores your horse is much less likely to become ill.

Dehydration

Dehydration, loss of body fluid, should always be taken very seriously but is not always obvious until a five per cent loss of body weight occurs. Once this rises to fifteen per cent the situation becomes life threatening and needs immediate veterinary intervention if it is not to have catastrophic consequences. Dehydration stresses the entire system so learning to recognize the signs is very important, these are:

- Tenting of the skin

- Weakness

- Dry mucous membranes

- Depression

- Sunken eyes

- Long capillary refill time

- Raised pulse

Once the horse has reached the stage of shock and circulatory collapse the situation is usually terminal.

Poor Nutrition

This is another situation that stresses the entire system. A proper balanced diet is needed to maintain all body tissues and for growth and repair. A horse that is badly nourished will find it very difficult to fight off 'run of the mill' infections and will be slower to heal any kind of injury.

Exposure to Infection

In the normal course of events exposure to some infections can be a good thing in that it allows the horse to build up his immunity but many skin diseases are easily passed on by contact with the infective agent. For that reason it is unwise to share tack or clothing especially if it has not been thoroughly cleaned first.

A classic example of a contagious skin disease passed on in this way is ringworm, the symptoms of which you will find later in the chapter. In a yard where hygiene is poor and tack and brushes are shared on a regular basis ringworm can spread like wildfire to the degree where all the horses are infected. If this happens on a large yard the process of cleaning it up and eradicating the infection is almost impossible with the added risk that any new horses coming onto the yard run the risk of also becoming infected.

Unsanitary Conditions

A stabled horse should always have a clean dry bed to sleep on as standing and lying on filth will very quickly have an adverse affect on his skin and feet. The skin itself is remarkably resilient but if it is constantly exposed to contamination by stale urine and faeces the surface will begin to break down resulting in ulcers and infections.

Dirty stable conditions also predispose the horse to an infection in the foot known as thrush. This is caused by an anaerobic bacteria which thrives in the clefts of the frog. The horse must have his feet cleaned daily and should have a clean dry bed.

Bad Housing

Apart from the obvious physical risks to the skin posed by protruding nails and broken doors, poor housing can be psychologically quite damaging for the horse. Stables that are very dark or have very low roofs can induce claustrophobia, which will be very stressful for the horse eventually leading to bad behaviour and failure to do well.

Lack of Routine

Most horses respond very well to routine and some of them react badly when their routine is disrupted whilst others appear not to care. Knowing what to expect and when to expect it definitely reduces stress in horses and as we have seen already stressful conditions contribute to circumstances that predispose disease.

Brutal Treatment

I sincerely hope that no readers of this book will ever brutalize a horse, however it is not unlikely that at some time they may have a horse that has been subject to brutal treatment in their charge.

Horses remember situations that have caused them pain and distress for a very long time and may carry the memory of it for their entire life.

Diseases of the Skin

Growths and Tumours

Like all animals horses can suffer with growths and these are, needless to say most noticeable when they involve the skin. Any growth will be either benign or malignant and this is usually determined by biopsy. Recommendations as to treatment are normally made on the basis of the laboratory findings.

Common skin growths in horses demonstrate the following nature:

- Sarcoid   Semi malignant

- Carcinoma   Malignant

- Melanosarcoma   Malignant

- Melanoma   Benign

- Fibroma   Benign

- Papilloma   Benign
- Squamous cell carcinama   Malignant

There are of course many other types of growths and tumours affecting other tissues and organ systems of the body, the list above refers only to those affecting the skin.

Warts and Sarcoids

Warts are types of tumours and are classed as the most common growths found in horses. There are three types of wart all of which are associated with viral infections and compromise of the immune system.

Viral papillomata or milk warts are caused by a virus similar to that producing warts in man and cross infection can occur though rarely does so. They are often passed from the mare to the foal during suckling but can be transmitted from foal to foal or by contact with infected material.

Milk warts are almost always confined to young horses less than eighteen months of age. They are usually found in clusters on the less hairy parts of the body like the muzzle, eyelids, nostrils and front legs although they can occur in other areas. In appearance they are small cauliflower-like, grey protuberances which are firm to the touch. They can be extensive round the mouth.

Equine papillomavirus has an incubation period of sixty days followed by a growth period of four to eight weeks after which the warts reach maturity. Once mature they usually disappear spontaneously within three to four

Papilloma on the muzzle.

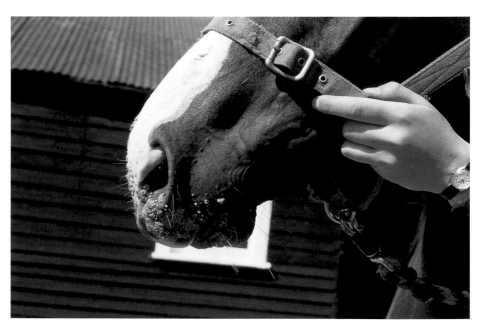

months after which immunity develops. As the condition is contagious young horses displaying symptoms should be isolated from others of the same age group. Similarly warts can be spread during mating so it is advisable not to breed from infected mares and stallions. The virus can persist in the environment in such places as stables, fences and clothing and at room temperature can live away from the host for at least three weeks. It can also be spread by contaminated brushes and hypodermic needles with transmission most likely to occur when the skin is scratched or punctured.

Occasionally warts become persistent spreading and appearing in unusual parts of the body. This may mean that the horse's immune system is not functioning fully or that the horse is suffering from a completely different problem. Under these circumstances a vet should be consulted.

Milk warts are a blemish but do not usually cause any problems unless they are located in an area where they may be subject to trauma (under tack) or in the event of them becoming secondarily infected. Diagnosis is usually by clinical appearance although this may be confirmed by biopsy. Milk warts are benign in characteristics.

Usually warts do not give cause for concern and do not require treatment. They can be surgically removed but excision of multiples can lead to considerable discomfort for the horse and on the soft, delicate skin of the muzzle, significant scarring. There are a variety of creams available but many of these are poisonous. When treating the muzzle there is a risk of the horse licking the treated area.

The second type of wart is a single protuberance from the skin that if left undisturbed and undamaged can remain unchanged for years. This type of wart is less common than the third type to which it is related, the sarcoid.

A sarcoid is a skin growth, usually affecting adult horses, which again is thought to be caused by a virus, possibly due to a previous non-productive infection. They are sometimes referred to as angleberries because of their large and multiple nature and can grow on all parts of the body particularly the inner thigh although occasionally the ear.

Sarcoids have the properties of benign tumours as they only form seedlings in their immediate surroundings but they also have malignant characteristics as they invade the skin and tend to recur after surgical removal. They can remain static for months or years having grown rapidly. Sarcoids start as small wart-like lumps covered in smooth, hairless skin. As they grow the skin covering the sarcoid changes becoming either thin and fragile, eventually breaking down to allow an ulcer to develop or becoming thick and horny. Rapid growth can also follow damage or trauma making sarcoids significant when they occur on stallions and are situated on the chest or sheath. The same problem arises with mares where the sarcoids are situated close to the udder and are knocked as the foal suckles.

Sarcoid.

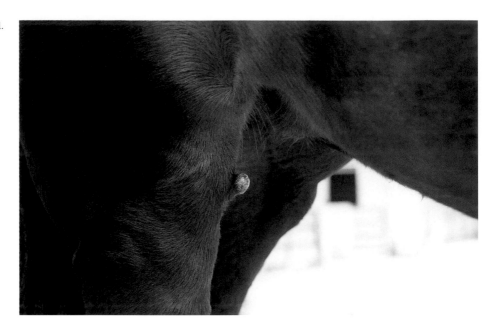

There are three types of equine sarcoid, verrucae (wart-like), fibroplastic and mixed, all of which may be squat or stalked. They occur most commonly in sites subject to trauma. Unlike milk warts they do not regress with age and because of their malignant characteristics may be detrimental when having a horse vetted for soundness.

Finally it sometimes happens that foals are born with congenital warts. The theory is that the infection can somehow cross the placenta to the embryo. These warts can occur in strange places such as the middle of the forehead, they are soft and rubbery to touch and darker in colour. As there is normally only one or two the vet can usually successfully remove them. Occasionally simple warts and sarcoids are confused with proud flesh resulting from penetrating wounds or the presence of foreign bodies such as splinters.

Conventional treatment for warts or sarcoids is usually by cytosurgery or surgical excision but care must be taken as sarcoids frequently reappear larger than ever following this type of treatment.

Melanoma

Melanomas are another relatively common tumour found in horses and are most usually seen in mature grey animals. Many animals remain unaffected by the presence of melanomas and go on to lead long and successful careers but for a few there are more serious consequences.

Usually melanomas are benign, slow growing tumours that present as firm black or grey masses occurring in various sites around the body. They are most usually located under the tail but can also be seen behind the jaw or under the ear. Occasionally they appear on the genitalia and even less frequently on the legs and neck and on the eyelid. Sometimes they occur in the eye itself.

Allergic Skin Diseases

Urticaria (hives)

Urticaria, sometimes called nettle rash or hives, is not usually a life threatening condition although a very severe case may interfere with the horse's breathing. It can be quite dramatic in appearance as lumps of varying sizes start appearing all over the horse's skin before running into each other to produce large areas of soft swelling. The lesions appear very rapidly and can also disappear in a matter of hours and if they don't you should call the vet.

Finding the cause of urticaria is frequently very difficult and in fact you may never find it, in medical terms this is called idiopathic. What we do know is that it is the result of an allergic reaction to something that the horse has been exposed to and been sensitized by. This can be any number of things from something that has been applied to the skin such as a shampoo or fly spray to insect bites. If you do manage to discover the allergen remove it immediately and make sure the horse does not have access to it again. In all cases the horse will have been exposed to the allergen at least once.

Common causes of urticaria include foods particularly compounded feeds containing animal protein, pollen, drugs and stress so when trying to establish what has caused the reaction all of these will need to be considered. Thin

Urticaria. Raised lumps on the neck caused by an allergic reaction.

skinned horses can be just as subject to nettle stings as we are, especially if they have inadvertently been rolling in a patch of nettles.

The lesions can appear anywhere on the body with the hair on the lesion sometimes being raised. They can be localized or cover large areas with a variety of oddly shaped lumps. There is no seepage of serum or blood and therefore no crust formation.

Many cases of urticaria spontaneously clear up without treatment and never recur but where it happens more than once it may indicate a more serious allergy that needs investigation by the vet.

If your horse does develop urticaria you should call the vet immediately if:

- There is a sudden appearance of extensive oedema.

- The horse is very agitated and upset.

- There is any sign of laboured breathing.

- The muzzle is very swollen.

- The eyes are very swollen.

- There is little or no sign of the swellings, other than the above, going down after twenty four hours.

Contact and allergic dermatitis

Dermatitis is an inflammatory skin condition caused by an outside agent with varying degrees of itchiness. It may result from a response to an allergen as in an allergic reaction or, as in the case of contact dermatitis, by direct skin contact with something the skin reacts to. In humans contact dermatitis is common amongst hairdressers who do not wear protective gloves when applying colourants or perm solutions to the hair. Once the skin has been sensitized to something the situation is permanent and cannot be reversed, that is to say that the skin will always subsequently be sensitive to that agent.

Resolution of the problem rests with the removal of the offending agent but as this is likely to be something that has been in the horse's environment for some time identification is not always easy.

Naturally occurring contact dermatitis in horses (in no particular order) has been known to be caused by:

- Medicines for example topically applied antibiotics.

- Pasture plants.

- Clothing and tack.

- Spray grooming aids.

- Shampoos, fly sprays and soap.

- Materials such as wool and jute.

Insect bites

Horses are pestered by a number of different types of flies but it is the biting flies that can stimulate an allergic reaction. The fly bites the horse in order to feed on blood and to do this successfully it injects its saliva to slow down the process of blood clotting thereby enabling it to feed for longer. It is the contents of the saliva that produce the allergic reaction.

In some horses this reaction can be extreme producing huge, extensive swellings. These can usually be identified as a fly bite by a raised lump with a hole in the centre somewhere around the middle of the swelling itself. They can take some time to go down and are a nuisance under the saddle or around the girth area.

The reaction to fly bite varies in severity from horse to horse with younger and recently introduced animals being more affected than horses that are older or have been in the vicinity for some time. Horses that suffer extreme reactions should be brought in during the day when the flies are most active and liberally sprayed twice a day or more with an appropriate fly spray. If this is not possible or practical, fly nets can be useful in keeping flies off providing the flies don't get trapped underneath them but the horse should also be sprayed.

Cleanliness in the field and stable and by this I mean the removal of droppings will help to restrict the breeding sites of the flies and thereby reduce the overall population.

Sweet Itch (Summer Seasonal Recurrent Dermatitis)

SSRD or Summer Seasonal Recurrent Dermatitis, also known more as Sweet Itch, is a common and miserable skin disease affecting roughly four per cent of horses and ponies in the UK. It is caused by an allergic reaction or hypersensitivity to the bite of a Culicoides midge, a tiny fly of which there are some twenty species in the UK. All horses are bitten by the midge but only some develop the hypersensitivity that results in the condition we identify as sweet itch. Animals which are predisposed to the development of sweet itch begin to show signs of it between one and four years of age with the condition becoming worse in the summer months. Commonly symptoms will first appear in the autumn. Mature animals that develop the disease are thought to do so because of stress factors such as moving to a new home with unfamiliar companions or incidents of injury or disease but by far the most important factors in the onset of sweet itch in any age group are environmental and indeed the main treatment of this disease is the management of these environmental factors.

Rubbing of the tail due to sweet itch.

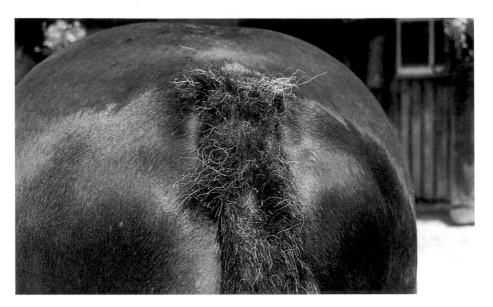

In the UK sweet itch is classed as an unsoundness which ought to be declared when the horse or pony is sold but every year winter-bought ponies surprise their new owners by developing the condition come late spring. Sweet itch is thought to be hereditary with some breeds of horses more prone to the disease than others, however it is rare in the English Thoroughbred.

This distressing condition is not a contagious disease although one or more animals in a field may present with the same symptoms, not surprisingly after all they are subject to the same environmental factors! It is by far the most common skin allergy in horses and ponies and occurs throughout the world where it is known variously as Queensland itch, summer itch, summer eczema and seasonal dermatitis.

If you suspect your horse or pony has sweet itch it is important to get a proper clinical diagnosis from your vet. Because of the seasonal nature of the disease this should not be difficult and will at least eliminate other causes of pruritus such as lice and ringworm.

Symptoms start to appear end of April to May time and persist until September or October although having said that, in a few very rare cases, they persist almost all year with last year's symptoms barely having cleared up before the onset of another bout the following spring.

Sweet itch is characterized by intense itching (pruritus) causing the horse or pony to vigorously rub or scratch the affected parts on anything they can get up against, if there is nothing convenient for them to rub on they may even pull themselves along the ground to scratch the belly or sit like a dog and wiggle round to scratch the tail. Sufferers frequently badger their field companions for extra mutual grooming or pace up and down continuously. Vigorous tail swishing or excessive rolling is also seen. Those unfortunate animals enclosed in electric fencing will resort to biting their flanks and the base of the tail and scratching the mane with a hind hoof.

Constant scratching and rubbing causes the skin to thicken and the hair to become broken and fall out and it is at this point that we may notice, if we have not already done so, that the horse has sweet itch. It is not uncommon for the condition to worsen with successive years until the skin becomes so damaged that hair no longer grows and the tail has a rat-tail appearance. Constant damage to the hair may result in it growing back white during the winter months so when buying a horse or pony in the winter keep an eye out for white hairs in the mane and tail root.

Other physical symptoms include flaky scurf and weeping sores, sometimes with a yellow crust of dried serum (Exudative dermatitis). Secondary infection can complicate things further if these sores are left untreated.

Apart from the physical signs the psychological impact on the horse's performance can be dramatic. For those poor animals that suffer from sweet itch it is a truly miserable experience. Imagine trying to do anything with an intense and constant itch somewhere you can't scratch – having suffered from eczema I know how they feel. If your horse or pony has sweet itch he needs your sympathy and your help in order to minimize his symptoms.

Symptoms of sweet itch will cause a horse to totally lose his ability to concentrate and lack any 'oomph' when working. You may also notice he is lethargic and yawns a lot or is cranky and impatient. Insects buzzing around, or anything that sounds like them for instance model aircraft, will produce general agitation and can set off a bout of head shaking. With all that to put up with it is not surprising that some horses also loose weight!

Sweet itch is caused by hypersensitivity to the bite of a tiny fly that is so small as to be able to pass through conventional mosquito netting. A local allergic reaction occurs to a protein in the saliva of the midge causing intense irritation. Basically the body's immune system over reacts to what is a harmless substance by attacking it's own skin cells and it is the damage caused by this attack that precipitates the symptoms of sweet itch. Sweet itch is therefore a problem of the immune system and as such is very difficult to deal with.

Culicoides midges mostly feed at dusk and dawn in calm warm conditions and they breed in wet conditions, rotting vegetation, water troughs and muck. Under the mane and at the root of the tail are the areas most affected along with the neck, ears, forehead, withers and across the rump but in severe cases the condition also appears along the mid-line of the belly, the saddle area, the sides of the head, the sheath or udder and the legs, in fact just about anywhere.

The key to this disease is of course accurate diagnosis and treatment with appropriate drugs but above all good management of the environment.

If the allergic reaction is severe, your vet can prescribe antihistamines and corticosteroids to minimize a bad reaction but these drugs will only bring temporary relief and carry the risk of various side-effects. Some owners have found a dilute solution of benzyl benzoate (available from the chemist) beneficial. Your vet will also advise on a suitable good management regime to ameliorate the problem but make no mistake the control of the problem is in your hands and the only way to successfully do this is to keep the culicoides midges away from the horse.

There are a number of measures you can take to do this. Firstly remove your horse from proximity to woodland, ponds, lakes, rivers, standing water or any other sources of wet ground or rotting vegetation as these are the breeding grounds of the fly. An ideal location to move him to, if possible, is an exposed windy site as the midges cannot cope with windy conditions. Rug the horse up with a lightweight rug that covers the belly and has a hood, fly nets won't do as the midge is so small it can get through mosquito netting. It will also help in the quest to keep the flies away from the horse to feed a fly repellent supplement such as garlic. Culicoides midges tend to feed on selected parts of the horse but topical application of fly repellents need to be applied all over, possibly twice a day, if they are to be of any use. For an all over treatment the best kind to use are the sponge on type with an application of pour on type on the worse affected areas. Make sure you read the instructions thoroughly first as there may be considerations with regard to mixing of different preparations. One other point regarding fly sprays, before you liberally plaster it all over your horse you will need to conduct a patch test to make sure there is no adverse reaction to any of the ingredients in the spray, you don't want to swap one irritant for another.

Essential oils are excellent natural substances to use for fly control and for making soothing anti-inflammatory creams and lotions. There are a number of good books which give instructions for making itch gels and fly repellents.

Another method of preventing the midge from feeding is to use an oil based product on the affected areas however this is messy. Soothing creams and lotions will reduce the itch for a while and stop your horse from rubbing quite so much. If possible he should be stabled over the times the midges habitually feed i.e. dawn and dusk and turned out only at night but you also need to pay attention to the stable environment. You will need to be able to close the doors and the window or fix very fine mesh/net over these openings to prevent an invasion by the midges. A great way to discourage them and keep them out is to provide a fan in the stable to circulate the air, this should be directed at the door to stop the midge flying in, however you must make sure it is securely fixed and well out of reach of your horse.

Having done all this and got the physical environment under control you will need to tackle the emotional and psychological aspects of the disease. Don't expect him to forget immediately what he has been going through or to understand that a windy field, summer rug and being brought in during the day equates to less itching. Scratching can become a habit and you need to break the itch scratch cycle.

Many people get the environment right and then forget that when they ride out the horse is once more exposed to the attentions of the midge. With this in mind it is as well to avoid riding in the vicinity of places where the midges breed and to remember to apply a good all over covering of fly repellent before taking him out for exercise.

With sweet itch there are no cures and definitely no quick fixes, even short time exposure to a few biting flies can result in three weeks of itchiness. Throughout the 'biting' season preventative measures must not be relaxed if the programme is to successfully control the condition. This is time consuming but must be adhered to if you are to get the best out of your horse. One further point, you should never breed from a horse with sweet itch.

Fungal Skin Diseases

Ringworm

Ringworm is a fungal skin disease that has nothing to do with any kind of worms. It gets its name from the small roundish patches of hair loss caused by a fungus. The most common species of ringworm are Trichophyton and Microsporum but there are a number of other less frequently seen varieties. The incubation period for ringworm is long and spores are able to persist in woodwork in stables and fences for over a year. This accounts for why some horses develop the disease after having moved into a stable that has not been used for some time. Young horses with less well developed immune systems and those that are undernourished are most at risk of infection.

Unfortunately there is not much you can do to actively prevent your horse getting ringworm but good stable hygiene goes a very long way to preventing the spread of the disease. Although ringworm is not painful and causes most horses very little discomfort, if you suspect your horse has ringworm you must isolate him immediately and call the vet. This is because ringworm is extremely contagious. It can manifest itself in a number of different guises so any unexplained skin lesion should be checked out for ringworm infection. Because of its aggressive nature it is one of the few conditions that it is worth treating anyway just in case infection is confirmed. However ringworm is itself self limiting and incidents of the disease are in most cases followed by spontaneous recovery.

There is one thing however that you must be aware of, equine ringworm is transmissible to humans. If, after dealing with a horse that has ringworm you develop a rash, consult a doctor immediately.

The initial stages of ringworm may present with just raised tufts of hair, these can be any shape, despite popular belief, and can be located anywhere on the body. The tufts of hair fall out leaving patches that may look red and sore, these patches may, classically, show as grey, scurfy or crusty areas of broken, damaged hair. In addition some horses become very itchy whilst others do not seem to be disturbed at all. Over the subsequent few weeks the hair will naturally grow back over the affected areas.

What should you do if you suspect your horse has ringworm? Firstly isolate him from any other horses and impose a strict hygiene routine to prevent the spread of the disease. Ringworm is spread by contact with infected items such as brushes, saddlery and rugs and by contact with woodwork where the disease has been lying dormant. The infected horse must have his own accommodation where he cannot touch other horses and his own grooming kit, rugs and tack.

Once the disease has been confirmed you will need to confine the spread and kill the fungus to prevent further environmental contamination. To do this you should wash your hands thoroughly, disinfect your boots and change any clothing that may have come into contact with the infected horse before dealing with other animals. Clipping and grooming should be abandoned until the infection has cleared up because of the risk of spreading the fungus spores. The disease can be allowed to run its course, which will take about four weeks, and the plus side to this is the horse will develop some immunity but this also allows the environment to become further contaminated and on balance it is preferable to kill off the fungus as quickly as possible.

Treatment is usually in the form of washes and lotions to be applied to the lesions. Stables must be thoroughly disinfected and the woodwork sprayed with a fungicide especially for the purpose, if possible bedding should be burnt. Rugs, grooming kits and tack must be disinfected or replaced.

Ringworm does not lead to death or severe debility.

A good example of a lesion caused by ringworm.

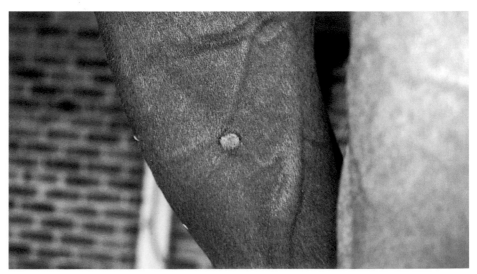

Bacterial Skin Diseases and Infections (Pyoderma)

Cellulitis

An infection of the deep dermis of the skin by steptococci bacteria. This is a diffuse, spreading inflammation of tissue and is a general term in as much as it can be around a tendon sheath, along a muscle or in the subcutaneous layer of the skin. Cellulitis may be purulent. Horses with cellulitis usually present with rapid onset swelling and lameness with no apparent cause. The condition can progress to necrosis (death of some of the tissue), sloughing and ulceration. Although the infection is located in the dermis this will sometimes extend to the epidermis and form draining tracts onto the surface.

Acne

This is sometimes referred to as saddle boils and is caused most frequently by a bacteria called *Staphylococcus aureus* that lives quite normally on the surface of the skin where it does not cause a problem. However, where the skin is dirty from lack of grooming and becomes abraded it enters the skin, giving rise to a pustular reaction. The presence of skin parasites and the use of dirty clothing and badly fitting tack all predispose the horse to a bout of acne. In a nutshell acne is caused by poor stable hygiene.

Once a diagnosis is confirmed treatment involves clipping the affected areas and cleaning with a mild antiseptic wash. Antibiotic cream is sometimes prescribed but stable hygiene must be improved if a reccurrence of the condition is to be prevented. Horses should be rested during treatment.

Lymphangitis

Strictly speaking lymphangitis is an inflammation of the lymph vessels and not a disease of the skin, however its appearance demonstrates with swelling and it can be ulcerative in nature which definitely involves the skin.

Lymphangitis is a bacterial infection of the cutaneous lymphatics i.e. the drainage system within the deeper layers of skin. Once again it is yet another skin disease associated with poor stable management but not all cases can be attributed to bad practice. Hind legs are more frequently affected than the fore and the swelling is usually confined to the lower part of the limb. In some cases, lymphangitis can lead to a permanently enlarged limb.

In severe cases the lymph oozes through the skin and drainage tracts onto the surface may form. These then develop into abscesses followed by ulceration, paving the way for yet further infection.

A horse with lymphangitis may have a raised temperature and the leg will

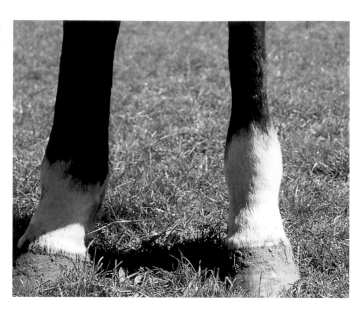

The thickened fetlock of a horse with lymphangitis.

be painful, discouraging movement which itself will exacerbate the situation by causing a further build up of fluid, and products from damaged tissue, leading to an increase in the pain.

Treatment is with antibiotics and painkillers with cold water hosing of the affected limb. Once the pain is under control the horse should be encouraged to move about which will speed recovery by improving the drainage to remove fluid and toxin and debris.

Mud fever, rain scald and cracked heels dermatophilosis streptothrycosis mycotic dermatitis (in America 'scratches')

Mud fever is one of the commonest skin complaints to affect horses and ponies. Cracked heels, rain scald and, in America, scratches are synonymous with mud fever as is the term 'greasy heels' found in older texts. It is characterized by inflammation and painful sores chiefly on the lower legs although it can affect any part of the body, including the belly and the neck that is subjected to wet, muddy conditions.

The diseases mud fever, cracked heals and rain scald are all caused by the same organism, a bacterium called *Dermatophilus congolensis*. Although *Dermatophilus*, meaning 'skin loving', is classified as a bacteria it has some fungal characteristics. It prefers areas which are lacking in oxygen and possibly high in carbon dioxide and it can be transmitted from horse to horse and to man. It lurks as a natural inhabitant of the soil and the hair of a horse's coat where it is always present, waiting for an opportunity to invade the skin. *Dermatophilus* can remain dormant for long periods of time in dry skin crust on the horse and his tack, and in the ground though it does not favour moist soil.

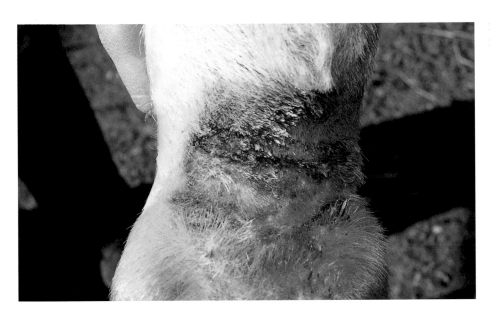

Lesions caused by
mud fever.

Despite its ever present threat you will be pleased to know that *Dermatophilus* cannot penetrate normal healthy skin.

The different common names applied to the disease can be confusing and this arises due to the condition manifesting on different parts of the horse's body. Rain scald appears on the rump, back, neck and head, cracked heals presents in the hollows of the pasterns and mud fever on the legs and belly.

The disease can affect stabled and grass kept horses and is seen both in horses with heavy feather and those with clipped legs. Horses with heavy feather are affected more often than those with clean legs. In some years there is a higher incident of the condition than in others and in some horses it can recur. Horses with white legs are particularly susceptible and some have less resistance to the disease than others. Although these diseases are commonly thought to be a winter thing in a susceptible equine they can occur in summer too. There is some thinking that horses grazed on pasture which has recently had cattle on it may be more prone to mud fever but this is only conjecture.

Once you know what to look for, mud fever is easy to spot though not always easy to deal with and, a word of warning, ignore it at your peril.

The first indication of a bout of mud fever that people usually notice is crusty scabs like lumps of dried mud on the affected areas and a lumpy feel to the surface of the skin. This is not the first sign of mud fever infection and serves to highlight how important it is to actively look for this disease on a daily basis. Initial signs of infection for mud fever and cracked heels are heat and itching with the hairs raised into a more upright position. For rain scald it is usually small areas of hair loss. There may also be some swelling in the area.

As the disease progresses unchecked inflammation will begin to spread to the subcutaneous tissue and in severe cases the bacteria will penetrate right through the skin and start to multiply underneath. Where the back of the pastern is involved the swelling stretches the skin which exudes serum and finally cracks horizontally. These cracks, typifying cracked heels, can be very deep and constant movement spreads them even further open. The cracks in the skin now allow entry of further bacteria leading to secondary infections and an increase in the clinical signs. Removal of the scabs will be painful for the horse (this is necessary as the scabs protect the bacteria from any treatment applied) and lumps of skin and hair will come away revealing a red sore area. There may also be heat and swelling, particularly of the legs, and the horse may be stiff in the gait or lame.

Basically mud fever occurs when the epidermis is compromised and the bacterium enters the skin. It is classified as a local dermatophilus infection and signs appear on and around the seat of infection. There are a number of predisposing factors, a combination of which lead to a bout of mud fever. These factors fall into two distinct groups, environmental and health related but strangely enough the one thing that is not necessary for your horse to get mud fever (although it definitely contributes) is the ubiquitous mud.

EnvironmentalFactors	*Health Factors*
Cold and wet	Stress
Mud	Lowered immunity
Bacteria	Damaged skin

Where the skin is always damp in prolonged wet muddy conditions it becomes softened (see the chapter on Functions and Structure of skin) and the protective sebaceous film of the epidermis is broken down and lost with continual wetting, grit in the mud abrades the skin as do ill-fitting rugs or halters, leading to wounds, however tiny, through which the bacteria can enter. Poor hygiene and bad management also play a large part in a horse's predisposition to mud fever.

The following is a scenario leading up to an attack of rain scald. A horse is caught out in the field in a hailstorm. As soon as he realizes the situation the horse's owner brings the horse into the stable where he puts a rug on him even though he is still wet. Under the rug the conditions are now warm and damp, perfect for bacteria to thrive in. The horse's back has been damaged by the hailstones allowing bacteria to enter the skin. Before long the owner finds he has a case of rain scald. Diagrammatically this is what usually happens;

Wet ➡ Dry ➡ Wet ➡ Dry ➡ Chapped Skin ➡ Entry of Bacteria

Infection

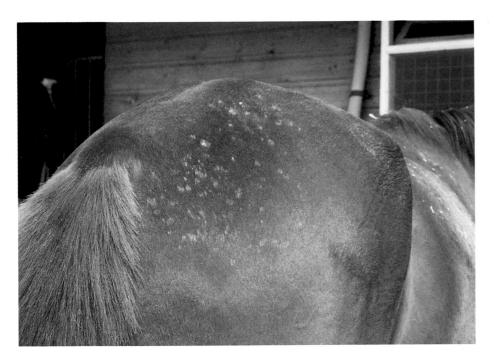

Typical appearance of rain scald.

It is of paramount importance that you take immediate action if your horse contracts mud fever. Failure to act quickly can lead to secondary complications and infections. The legs can become swollen with open sores that are difficult to heal and your horse may be lame. It can take months for a horse to recover from a severe bout of mud fever. There may be permanent hair loss and proud skin and, in extreme cases, it may be necessary to use skin grafts.

An outline plan of treatment can be divided into three stages following the removal of all the predisposing factors of cold, wet, stress and infective agent.

1. Kill the bacteria.
   Use any antiseptic that kills bacteria Good antibacterial agents to use are Napisan, Iodine, or Hibiscrub.

2. Soothe and heal the wounds.
   Demobion, witchhazel, aloe vera, myrrh, tea tree oil, manuka honey (activated), vitamin E creams.

3. Protect the area from further damage.
   Use good quality barrier creams.

If you see signs of mud fever on your horse the first thing you must do is to remove him from the cause that is get him out of the predisposing environment, the wet and mud. If possible he should be relocated to a clean and dry stable but if this is not feasible at least get him onto dry ground.

Firstly deal with the environmental factors. Carefully clip the hair from the affected area taking care not to cut the skin. Wash the area with warm water and an antiseptic and dry thoroughly. Scabs should be gently removed but this can be very painful for the horse and they may need softening first using warm water or an antiseptic cream. Washing the area and removing scabs needs to be done on a daily basis as the scabs form very rapidly. Having removed all the scabs the area can look very inflamed and sore. Apply a soothing antibiotic ointment such as Demobion to the area. Demobion contains a corticosteroid that helps reduce inflammation but it is only available from a vet. If there is a possibility of bedding sticking to the infected area it should be bandaged over a clean wad of gamgee however it is preferable to leave it open to the air if circumstances and the environment allow. After a few days of this treatment the area should be significantly less inflamed, the sores should have begun to heal and the hair to grow back.

In more severe cases it may be necessary to poultice the area, this will help to draw out the remaining bits of dirt and infection and the heat of the poultice will increase circulation and thus promote healing but where a secondary infection has become established a course of antibiotic therapy may be needed. Essential oils are extremely powerful against mud fever (see the chapter on Complementary Therapies) but should only be used to support any treatment your vet may prescribe and then only by a qualified practitioner.

Alongside the environmental causes of mud fever we also have to deal with the predisposing health factors. It is not always easy to work out why your horse is stressed or has reduced immunity.

Keeping your horse out of persistent wet and muddy conditions will go a long way to preventing a bout of mud fever although some horses are so susceptible to the disease that even splashing through muddy puddles whilst out hacking will bring on an attack. There is also controversy about washing or hosing off legs when bringing in from a muddy field or after a day's hunting. Personally I never wash my horse's legs unless I can wash them absolutely clean and dry them thoroughly preferring instead to provide them with a good deep bed of absorbent material and to brush the mud off with a soft brush once it is dry. If your horse shows no sign of having mud fever it is as well to leave their legs alone neither washing nor brushing the mud off but this is just a personal preference although I have to say that despite wet conditions and mud my horses do not have mud fever.

To prevent gateways and fields becoming too poached rotate them and where this is not possible make sure your horse does not spend most of his time knee deep in mud. Barrier creams such as zinc oxide and powders are available to help prevent mud fever but these tend to wear off as the horse moves round the paddock and if applied to semi-clean legs can actually make the situation worse by sealing in the bacterium. Some experienced owners still use that old fashioned remedy goose grease and very good it is too. If your horse has a lot

Equine chaps for turn-out. These have been developed to help combat mud fever. They help keep horses' legs clean, warm and mud-free. The chaps encase the horse's lower leg in breathable Stomatex, fitting over the hoof and under the heel.

of feather and is prone to mud fever trim this off as this holds the wet against the legs, however clipping the legs is not a good idea.

With mud fever, cracked heels and rain scald vigilance is the watch word. If you do decide to wash your horse's legs after exercise or when bringing in from the field do so with cold water, warm water will only soften the skin more and the warmth will create an environment in which the bacteria can thrive.

Skin Parasites

Skin parasites tend to cause more trouble in the winter months when horses are stabled or have long winter coats as, as well as protecting the horse at this time of year, the dense coat provides a wonderful environment for a variety of these hangers on.

In general skin parasites prefer the cooler weather and deep in the coat they are away from the dehydrating affects of the sun's rays. For instance a surface-feeding mite called *Chorioptes bovis* causes leg mange, which is always worse in winter. Irritation produced by their feeding habits characteristically leads to the development of foot stamping behaviour particularly in heavily feathered horses.

There is no doubt that horses that have shown no sign of skin disease previously, frequently develop itchiness and soreness for no apparent reason after being brought into the stable. Then having struggled with the problem all winter, the bemused owner finds the condition spontaneously disappears once the horse is turned out again in spring. In all probability the condition has been caused by some kind of minute skin parasite easily harboured in bedding and clothing that is not regularly washed.

Biting and chewing lice

Horses can be infested by both biting and chewing types of lice, both of which spend their entire lives, from eggs to adults, on the horse. Lice are flat insects with six legs and no wings that live on the surface of the skin. The biting variety, *Haematopinus asini*, are slightly larger and have more pointed heads than the chewing species, *Damalinia equi*, both are passed by direct contact from horse to horse or if the conditions are warm and moist, by contaminated clothing and tack.

Biting lice tend to favour the areas with longer hair like the mane, the tail and the fetlocks where they penetrate the skin with their mouth parts and suck blood and tissue fluids. They can however spread across the whole body.

The yellowy-brown chewing lice prefer areas of shorter hair like the flanks where they live on dead skin and surface debris, as with the biting lice, in a serious infestation, they can spread over the entire body.

As with most skin parasites lice prefer the colder times of year and populations can very easily build up during the winter months if left unchecked. They are very irritating to the horse and the biting variety can avail themselves of a

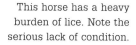

This horse has a heavy burden of lice. Note the serious lack of condition.

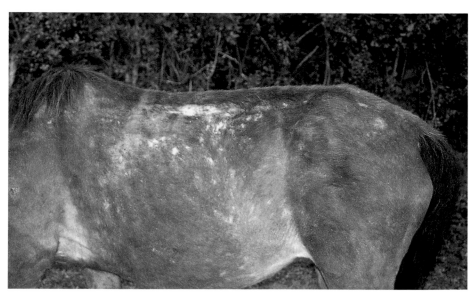

significant amount of blood. Heavy infestations are usually seen in winter amongst underfed horses with unkempt coats, and these are not infrequently only kept out at grass. Paleness of the mucous membranes due to blood loss and lack of condition accompanied by a scruffy ill-kempt coat are good indications of a serious infestation as lice can really drag a horse down in condition if not dealt with promptly.

On inspection the biting lice are much easier to see especially after they have been feeding when they will turn a bluish colour. The chewing lice, being smaller, are more difficult to see but close examination of the skin will reveal them moving away from the light. Treatment is with an appropriate insecticide thoroughly rubbed into the coat and followed with a second application two weeks later to kill any lice that have hatched since the first treatment.

If one horse in the stable has lice it is likely that the others have them as well so all horses in the yard should be treated at the same time and their clothing thoroughly cleaned before being used again.

Mites

Mites are microscopic skin parasites and they can live on the skin of the horse, in the skin or originate from somewhere else entirely.

Leg mange

Also called tail mange, foot mange, and symbiotic scab. The mites which cause leg mange, *Chorioptes equi*, live on the surface of the skin predominantly on the fetlock and back of the pasterns. Occasionally they spread up the legs and can be found on the belly, the tail and in the groin area. The mites feed by puncturing the skin and sucking tissue fluid which forms a dried crust on the surface of the leg. Under the crust the skin is red and inflamed and the lesions formed are very itchy leading the horse to stamp and scratch himself on any convenient surface. There is also loss of hair. This particular species of mite is very fast moving.

Diagnosis is by skin scraping taken from a lesion by a vet and examined under a microscope. Treatment is with an acaricide wash which needs to be repeated twice more at intervals of ten days. This is to ensure a complete kill of the mites, however if the treatment is not effective it should be repeated using a different acaricide wash. Draught horses with heavy feather are most likely to be affected.

Nodular mange

There is no information about how widespread this condition is as the mites causing it live deep in the hair follicles in the skin. Fortunately it is rarely seen but in all probability all horses are infected, they just don't display the symptoms. When symptoms are seen they take two forms, in the first the skin becomes thickened and scaly with hair loss over the head, neck and withers whilst in the second nodules containing a substance of a cheesy consistency develop over the face, neck and shoulders. The mites themselves are microscopic, cigar shaped organisms and diagnosis is by deep skin scrapings.

Trombicula

Also called harvest mite, scrub itch mite, chiggers and heel bug. These mites are free living in the soil of low-lying pasture and arable land. They are more common and seem to prefer free draining sandy or chalky soils. The eggs are laid in the soil and once hatched the larvae feed on the tissue fluids of small mammals although they are not host specific.

Horses are at most risk of attack after the harvest in late summer or autumn when the larval stage attaches itself around the heel and the pastern. Once attached they suck tissue fluid which dries to form a crust over reddened skin. These mites are so irritating that the horse is at risk of damaging himself in an effort to deal with the itch. On removal of the crust the mites can usually be seen as little orange dots embedded in the skin. Fortunately they are easily killed by bathing the legs with an anti parasitic wash. The only prevention is to keep horses away from areas where the mite is known to be common.

Fleas

Fleas are not significant parasites of horses.

Mange

Fortunately the most aggressive parasitic types, Sarcoptic and psoroptic mange, were eradicated from the UK in 1948.

Flies

Horses are frequently attacked by flies that are quite happy to bother other animals and humans as well to get their meal. Horses are pestered by a number of different flies that cause worry and irritation with subsequent loss of condition if the situation is not addressed. Some flies are attracted to the secretions from the eyes and other body orifices whilst others bite and feed on blood.

The situation is much worse in the warm, summer months when the flies are breeding and the severity of the problem will depend on the proximity to the insect's breeding ground. The mouth parts of the nuisance flies are designed for licking the secretions from the surface of the skin, mainly around the eyes and the nose but they are also attracted and make use of open wounds. Biting flies pierce the skin and feed on blood. The fly bites themselves can be painful but to overcome the body's own defences the fly injects saliva containing, amongst other things, an anti-coagulant to prevent the blood from clotting and allowing the fly to continue feeding. Many horses are allergic to the substances in the saliva (see insect bites in the section on allergies) and can suffer quite extreme reactions.

Flies, either nuisance or biting, also spread disease from horse to horse either on their feet or as parasitic organisms found in their saliva.

Horse flies

The horse fly bite is very painful, you will know this if you have ever been bitten by one, and they are easily recognized by their large size, sandy-brown colour and brightly coloured eyes. They are frequently seen in the open on hot, heavy days although some species prefer woodland and they breed in mud and water.

Once a horse fly has begun feeding it does not like to move far when disturbed and will try to settle on the same horse to continue. If this is not possible it will move to one very close to finish feeding. Horses will always try to move away from these flies and will rapidly lose condition if under constant attack.

Horse flies transmit equine infectious anaemia (EIA) from one horse to another by carrying the virus on their mouth parts. This can be prevented by grazing horses separately and by separating paddocks. However EIA was eradicated in the UK in 1976 although it remains a notifiable disease.

Stable flies

These biting flies are greyish in colour and breed in stable muck and dirty bedding. They are commonly seen during the day on the walls and windows of stables. Again the bite is quite painful and they will bite the same horse several times or move to the next horse to finish feeding. Horses become restless swishing their tails and stamping their feet as these flies can be extremely annoying.

A horse which is repeatedly bitten by stable flies will have little crusts over the back, shoulders and neck. The flies can transmit a number of diseases including Trypanosoma, a disease not found in the UK and Habronema (summer sores) which is. Stable flies also bite humans and dogs.

House flies

House flies come into the category of nuisance flies as they feed on the secretions around the eyes and the nose and on wounds. For preference they breed in horse manure and are therefore common in stables where they can be very irritating to horses if numbers are allowed to build up. The irritation produced by the flies around the eyes leads to extra tear formation which attracts even more flies to the area with consequent further damage to the eyes.

House flies can transmit conjunctivitis from one eye to the other and spread it to other horses. They can also spread summer sores. Prevention of the spread of disease is helped by fly masks.

Black flies

These are small flies that breed near water and fortunately there are not very many of them in the UK although they are very much more common in hotter climes. They will attack horses grazing near water particularly on warm, sultry days. The bite of the fly is painful causing a small nodule full of fluid. This blister is caused by a toxin that is injected into the horse by the fly and it is fortunate that the fly is not common in this country as a swarm of these flies biting a horse can inject enough toxin to kill it.

Culicoides

See sweet itch in the section on allergies.

Warble

Due to the government eradication programme, warble flies are now, fortunately, comparatively rare in horses. Years ago it was not uncommon to see a horse suddenly start up from grazing and gallop to the other end of the field for no apparent reason. In all probability the horse had heard a warble fly coming and knew what it was in for. The warble fly lays its eggs under the skin along the back where they eventually hatch into grubs. Model aircraft sound much like warble flies which is why so many horses are startled by them.

Bot flies

These flies look like rather dumpy bees with yellow banding, the ovipositor resembling a sting in the female. The flies hover around horses waiting for an opportunity to dart in and deposit eggs and are most active in late summer and autumn. Most horse people are familiar with the larval phase of the bot fly life-cycle which takes place in the stomach of the horse. In the UK most horses are infected. The eggs are easily seen on the legs and neck in groups of what look like small seeds sticking to the coat of horses out at grass and are easily removed with a bot knife specially made for the purpose.

The eggs of the bot fly are transferred to the mouth by the horse licking the eggs off his or another horse's coat, usually the legs, mane and neck. Having been transferred to the mouth, the eggs hatch and hang around for a month in the tissues of the tongue and gums, particularly round the molars, before being swallowed. A high burden of bots in the gut can do considerable damage and in some cases even lead to death if the stomach wall is perforated.

The adult flies are killed off by cold weather so from the point of view of control it is important to understand that during the winter the entire population of bot flies exists as larvae within the guts of horses. Removal of eggs

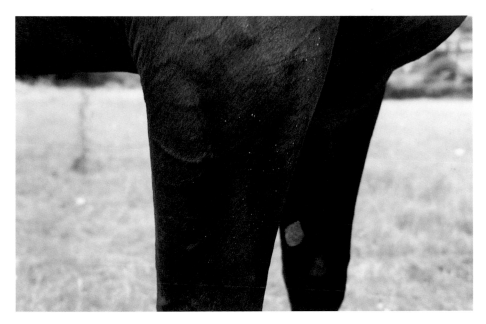

The yellow speckles on this horse's fore leg are bot fly eggs. These will be transferred to the mouth when the horse scratches himself. Once in the mouth the eggs hatch and the larvae burrow into the tissues of the tongue and gums, particularly round the molars. After about a month they are swallowed to continue the lifecycle in the gut. As many as possible should be removed with a bot knife.

from the coat and a good worming programme will reduce the incidence of bot flies in the following season.

Blowflies

This group of flies includes the blue-bottle, green-bottle and flesh flies, they are attracted to wounds where they lay their eggs. If left unattended the eggs hatch into maggots that invade and feed on the surrounding living flesh. This is done by dissolving the flesh into a sort of soup that the maggot is able to consume, needless to say it is very irritating for the horse who will become restless, swishing his tail and stamping, and a foul smelling discharge will begin to ooze from the wound.

Treatment involves removal of all the maggots and the application of insecticide to kill any that might remain. But prevention in this case is very much better than cure. All wounds must be thoroughly cleaned as soon as they are noticed and either covered and or treated with a suitable fly repellent to prevent fly strike.

Onchocerciasis

There are two types of *Onchocerca*, one which lives in the skin, neck and sometimes the eyes of horses (*O. cervicalis*) and one that infects the tendons and suspensory ligaments of the front legs. It is likely that all horses are infected but that the condition only presents itself when the animal develops a sensitivity or allergic reaction to the microfilariae or first stage larvae in the skin.

The adult worms lay the microfilariae that then migrate to the skin. They have a tendency to collect in the chest and lower abdomen and from these areas they are then picked up by feeding culicoides midges. Within the midge the first stage larvae grow to third stage larvae and are eventually transferred when the midge bites another horse. Having been transferred they migrate to the ligaments of the neck and grow into adults, life-cycle complete.

Most horses never show signs of infection but those that are sensitive to the worms may develop skin lesions. This hypersensitivity is thought to be brought on by an immune reaction to the microfilariae dying in the skin. The lesions are very itchy and the horse may injure himself by biting and scratching. Diagnosis is difficult as a number of other parasites produce skin lesions in the horse and only a few animals show a reaction to the worms whilst it is nearly always present. On top of this, as the reaction is likely to be due to the worms dying, to kill them off in large numbers will make the situation much worse in the short term. It is relatively easy to kill this parasite but large numbers dying off at once can produce oedematous swelling which will need to be treated with anti-inflammatories.

Viral Skin Diseases

Viral Papiloma

See the section on warts and sarcoids in Growths and Tumours.

Immune Mediated Disorders

Pemphigus Foliaceous

There are a number of different forms of *Pemphigus* but *Pemphigus foliaceous* is the most common and it is also the most common autoimmune dermatosis in the horse. It is likely that the onset of the disease is triggered by some event or stressful situation. Lesions may first appear on the face or legs and over the next few months can become generalized although in some cases the lesions are localized to the face or coronary band. There may be associated oedema and the horse may be itchy or in pain. Primary lesions are usually visicles, pustules or bullae but these are fragile and transitory so what is normally seen is anullar crusts and alopecia with varying degrees of weeping and scaling.

The early lesions in some horses are seen as tufted papules distributed over the withers and saddle area whilst in others there is extensive exfoliative dermatitis with no distinct sign of primary or secondary lesions. The condition is made worse by warm, humid, sunny weather. Horses with *Pemphigus foliacious* may be lethargic and depressed, they may lose their appetite and consequently, weight and they may also have a fever.

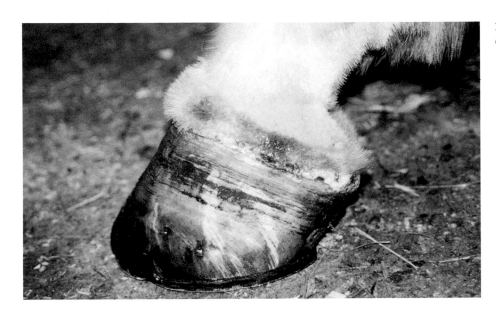

Pemphigus on the coronary band.

Very occasionally this disease will spontaneously resolve but this is a very rare occurrence and most horses need aggressive treatment to control it. Young horses respond better to treatment than older horses and have been known to stay in remission once treatment has been withdrawn. Treatment is usually with oral prednisolone which should be continued until the disease becomes inactive.

In some cases horses remain in remission following treatment but in others there may be relapse and treatment needs to begin again. In multiple incidences of relapse and remission treatment becomes progressively less effective. Horses should be kept out of the sun and in a cool place to reduce the incidence of sweating and associated itchiness.

Congenital and Hereditary Disorders

The average horse owner it not likely to encounter the following diseases as they are either extremely rare or the foals die before or quite soon after birth, however I have included information on them in case it is required.

Hypotricosis

Horses with *hypotricosis* have less than the usual amount of hair to the extent that they can be almost bald although in some cases the hairlessness is localized. Very little is known about this disease as it is extremely rare. Horse with *hypotricosis* may be healthy in all other respects but they are more susceptible to sunburn. They and their parents should not be bred from as the condition is thought to be hereditary.

Epitheliogenesis imperfecta

A very rare congenital disorder where the skin fails to fuse properly and the epidermis, dermis and subcutaneous adipose tissue may all be missing. In some cases single layers are absent. Foals may be born with some or all of the hooves missing and usually die within the first few days. Because the condition is caused by a recessive gene neither of the parents should be used again for breeding.

Lethal dominant white

This condition is caused by a dominant gene. The gene produces a white foal with either blue or hazel eyes, those that are homozygous die in utero from unknown causes with those that are born alive necessarily being heterozygous. By the law of averages mating two heterozygous white horses will result in a twenty five per cent mortality rate.

Albinism

Albinism is a genetic pigmentary abnormality. Albino horses are unable to produce melanin and therefore have no colour in the hair, skin or mucous membranes which are referred to as amelanotic. Usually they are also lacking colour in the iris so their eyes appear pink. Albino horses are usually sensitive to bright light but are normal in all other respects.

White foal syndrome

Not to be confused with the lethal dominant white, the gene that causes this condition is recessive. Foals that are white with blue eyes are born but die within a few days due to obstruction of the large intestine. Neither parent of this type of foal should be bred from.

Miscellaneous Skin Diseases

Photosensitization

Photosensitivity is the abnormal reaction of the skin to sunlight, fortunately it is not all that common although it affects both young and old horses. It is also called bluenose and it results from the ingestion or application of a photosensitizing agent or from liver damage resulting in poor elimination of the breakdown products of chlorophyll, the green colouring in plants, both of which cause the skin to become sensitized to the rays of the sun.

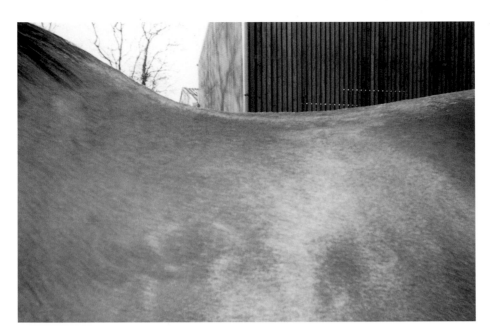

Undiagnosed nodular lumps on the back of this horse can be seen as raised areas of hair.

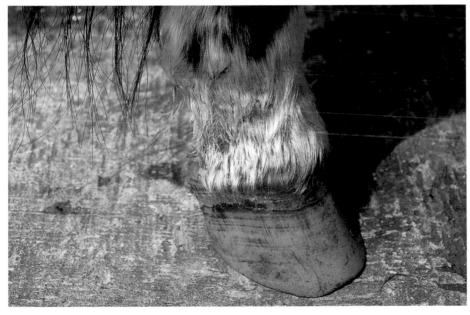

An example of photosensitization on a white pastern.

The condition occurs in bright sunny weather and the first areas to be affected in a case of photosensitization are areas where the hair is sparsest and where the skin in unpigmented, for example the muzzle. If the damage is widespread any large patches of skin with white hairs may be affected. Look for signs of increased sensitivity with the horse twitching his ears and rubbing his body. As the condition progresses the area first becomes reddened and then purplish, oedema of the underlying skin may also be present. After several days the skin of the affected areas may slough off to reveal the dermis underneath.

Photosensitization due to liver damage is likely to have a poor outcome, however if it is due to topical application or ingestion of a phototoxic substance it should be possible to treat the condition.

Dealing with the problem involves removing the horse immediately from exposure to the sun and housing him in a darkened stable. If you suspect photosensitization you must call the vet as the situation is unlikely to resolve itself. Where the skin has sloughed off treat the areas with an antiseptic powder and be extremely vigilant in checking for eggs deposited by flies. Phototoxic substances include St John's Wort (*Hypericum perforatum*) and bergamot essential oil.

Sweat lumps

The technical name for this skin condition is necrobiosis or nodular skin disease. The fibrous nodules appear under the skin and as they are not uncommonly in the saddle area are sometimes confused with pressure sores caused by badly fitting tack. As well as the saddle area sweat lumps are frequently found on the neck and shoulders.

The lumps themselves can be up to two centimetres in diameter and are not usually painful. There is some controversy as to what causes them, possible causes being a response to a stage in the life-cycle of a skin parasite known as *Onchocerca cervicalis* and an allergic reaction to some antigen.

Sweat lumps do not usually cause any problems, unless they appear under the saddle, but they are unsightly and can be difficult to get rid of. In a few horses they spontaneously regress but in most they persist. Conventional treatment involves either surgical removal or steroid injections into the nodules themselves but it is possible to treat this condition homoeopathically to disperse the fibrous material in the lumps. Where there is doubt diagnosis can be confirmed by biopsy.

Non parasitic mites

Forage mites live in hay and straw and can be found in large numbers in areas of the stable where fallen food had been allowed to accumulate. They cause intense itchiness in horses with subsequent self-excoriation and loss of hair. Usually they affect the head and neck in horses fed from high level hay racks or nets but they can migrate across the whole body.

Examination of material taken from an affected area of skin will reveal the presence of the mites when examined under a microscope or high power lense. Treatment with an anti-parasitic wash will remove the mites from the surface of the skin but it is important to find and deal with the root cause in order to prevent re-infection.

Forage mites cannot live on the horse but browse on the surface debris of the skin causing irritation. Feeding hay from the floor will rapidly improve the situation but the stable must be thoroughly swept and it would be wise to change the bedding if the infestation is severe.

Skin Trauma

Overreach

An overreach is when the hind hoof strikes into the back of the pastern of the foreleg and as you can imagine this can cause big problems if the horse is shod. There is laceration of varying depth and bruising of the surrounding area. Overreach injuries should be thoroughly cleaned and an antibiotic spray or wound powder applied. Avoid ointments as these can trap dirt next to the open wound with the subsequent risk of infection. It goes without saying that if the horse is lame he should not be worked. Until satisfactory healing has taken place the wound must be kept dry and clean and, depending on the circumstances, it may be better to keep the horse in until healing has taken place. To prevent further occurrence the horse should wear overreach boots during exercise.

Saddle sores, girth galls and sitfasts

These types of skin trauma are caused by constant pressure, which need only be light, and rubbing of the affected area by clothing and tack. Saddle sores and girth galls occur under the saddle and girth areas whilst sitfasts are nasty corn-like patches down the centre of the spine.

If the situation is not recognized and corrected there will be loss of hair followed by swelling, thickening of the skin, depigmentation and eventually ulceration. Destruction of the pigment cells in the skin is permanent and ever after the hair in the damaged area will grow white, this is known as acquired leukoderma and is an adventitial mark which must be recorded on the horse's identification papers.

Prevention is simple, make sure your tack fits, is always clean and that there is no dirt trapped between the horse and the tack.

Sunburn

Horses, like people, can be burnt by the sun and prevention is by either application of a sunblock or by bringing the horse in, out of the sun during the day. Animals with pink skin around the muzzle are most at risk and the area can become very sore. Treatment is with soothing creams and, to prevent any

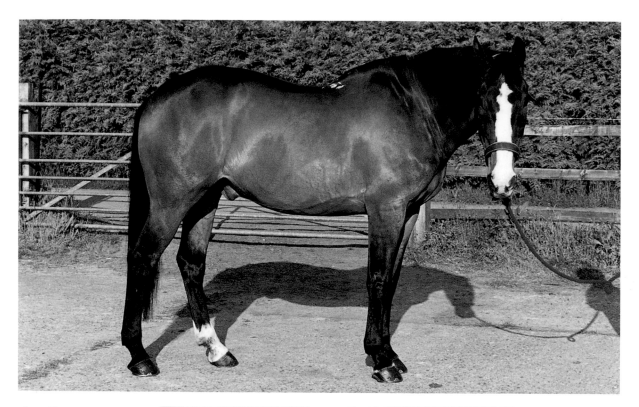

above The white marks just behind this horse's withers are indicative of saddle sores from badly fitting tack.

right Flesh coloured areas are particularly prone to sunburn and although it frequently goes unnoticed, many horses suffer during the summer months. The crusty bits on the muzzle are due to this pony having been sunburnt on a very hot spring day that took everybody by surprise. Use of a good sunblock on the flesh coloured parts will help to prevent this.

further incidence the use of a high factor sunblock. Lavender essential oil is excellent for all kinds of burns and can be applied neat to small areas.

Conditions Affecting the Skin

Cushing's Disease

The medical term for Cushing's disease is *hyperadrenocorticism*, it is predominately a disease of older equines with ponies being more at risk than horses. Although this is not primarily a skin disease one of the most striking aspect of Cushing's disease is the effect on the coat. This typically becomes long thick and shaggy (*hypertrichosis*) although the mane and tail are unaffected. Affected horses may show incomplete shedding and early re-growth of the coat and they are also more susceptible to skin infections.

General Debility

Poor condition and general debility will show in the coat which will be harsh, tight and staring. This may follow a period of inadequate nutrition, a heavy worm burden or an illness that has led to general debility but as the plane of nutrition improves and the horse gradually regains his strength the condition of the coat and skin will recover.

Toxicity

Selenium

Chronic selenium poisoning gives rise to emaciation, loss of the long hairs of the mane, tail and feathers, lameness and changes in the hoof such as vertical cracks and rings. The coat becomes rough and the hair of the mane and tail breaks easily. It can take several months for a horse to recover from selenium toxicity.

Iodine

This usually happens because of over-supplementation. Clinical signs include nasal discharge, cough, and joint pain. Changes to the skin are characterized by severe scaling over the back, head, neck and shoulders and in some cases there is a degree of alopecia. Iodine is naturally eliminated from the body during normal metabolism so once the offending items are removed from the diet, recovery is very rapid.

Miscellaneous

Intertrigo

This occurs where two skin surfaces are in juxtaposition and rub against each other along with moist conditions and an accumulation of debris. This sets up a superficial inflammatory dermatosis. Eventually the stratum corneum breaks down and secondary infection sets in. Gentle cleaning with antiseptics and a dusting of powder to reduce the friction will encourage healing which will take about three to four weeks.

Haematoma

Haematoma are most usually seen as a result of sudden external trauma and are formed by bleeding into surrounding tissue under the skin. In appearance they can be startling as they look like large swellings. They are rapid in onset and may or may not be painful. Some haematoma resolve themselves and do not need any treatment but others require surgical incision, evacuation of the contents and repair.

9.

Hygiene, First Aid and Treatments

If in doubt call the vet.

Skin and Stable Hygiene

Keeping a horse's skin free from disease is not something that happens by chance, it requires vigilance and attention to detail. When something does go wrong ask yourself is there anything you could have done differently to prevent it and be honest with your answer.

Cleanliness in the Stable

Poor stable hygiene and management are major contributory factors in the onset of many diseases so if your horse does become sick examine your routine to see if anything needs improvement. A horse kept in filthy conditions will inevitably be at risk from disease of one sort or another. Under these conditions even minor cuts or grazes can very easily become infected and when proper skin and coat care are neglected it is easy for the accumulation of debris, and other things normally found on the surface of healthy skin, to build up causing irritation and possibly exacerbating an existing skin condition.

Good stable hygiene starts with mucking out. A horse needs a warm, dry, clean bed to lie on at night and to maintain this we need to manage the bed properly. I don't propose to give a lesson in mucking out here, suffice it to say that that the surface of the bed must be dry and clean as bacteria and mould proliferate in damp, dirty conditions. At the very least all droppings and wet patches must be removed daily and clean fresh bedding added to the bed.

Managing the Muck Heap

Muck heaps should be located away from the stables and grazing as these provide an ideal breeding ground for a number of parasitic flies. Don't allow stagnant, filthy surface water or piles of muck to hang around in the yard or lurk in unswept corners. There is an art to managing a muck heap that it is well worth cultivating. Each day the fresh muck should be thrown up on the top and stood down, this involves jumping up and down on the top to compact it, this will keep the midden within acceptable boundaries and it will look a whole lot neater too.

Although a sufficient distance from the stables this muck heap is totally unmanaged and as a consequence has encroached on the car parking area. With a bit of effort it could be kept neat and tidy, fortunately it is removed completely on a regular basis.

Equipment

To keep the skin clean and promote health, regular grooming is a must. This is primarily done to keep the skin free of accumulations and debris that may predispose the onset of diseases. Any patches of scurf found should be dealt with immediately by brushing it off the skin and out of the coat.

Some skin diseases such as ringworm are very contagious and can exist in woodwork for a very long time. It is primarily spread from horse to horse by poor stable hygiene practices such as sharing rugs and brushes. It can spread throughout a yard extremely rapidly and because of this each horse should have his own set of brushes and rugs which are used on him only.

There is a deplorable trend nowadays for owners to have only one rug for inside and one to turn out in. This means that after the first week the horse is wearing dirty clothing. This is not good stable hygiene and on balance I think it is better to have several cheaper rugs than only one good one. This way they can be washed regularly and the horse always has a clean one to wear. Some modern stable rugs are light enough to put in a domestic washing machine,

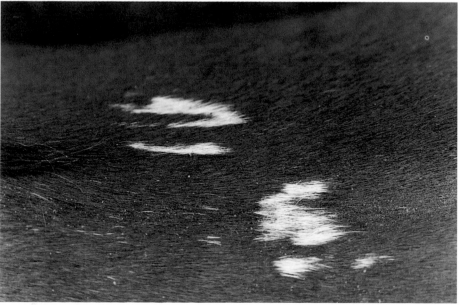

above Stagnant water provides an excellent breeding ground for all sorts of undesirable, potentially harmful creatures and organisms. A good crop of weeds is also flourishing where they shouldn't.

left Good, regular grooming would soon remove the scurf from the coat of this otherwise healthy horse.

169

my own horses that are not clipped, wear fleeces that are nice and cosy, wash well and dry really quickly.

Bandages should be washed, dried and properly stored every time they are used although stable bandages can probably be used a few times before they need to be washed if they are used, as they should be, over wadding, it all depends on how dirty they get. One thing you must never do is to use a dirty bandage to bind a wound.

It is also very important to keep boots clean. These tend to become crusty with sweat and grit which must all be brushed off completely before they are used again. Neoprene, a material popular for making boots, takes on the qualities of sandpaper if sweat is allowed to dry on the surface and is not cleaned off, next to a horse's skin this can cause unpleasant rubbed areas very quickly that can then become infected.

To keep the horse's skin clean you will need to have clean brushes. Many people don't wash their grooming kit from one year end to the next, apart from being a not very nice practice this is down right dangerous. Parasites, bacteria and fungi can all colonise brushes in amongst the dirt, grease and dead skin that accumulates in them. All items of the grooming kit should be regularly washed in warm soapy water with a dash of disinfectant before being thoroughly rinsed and dried. Unless your brushes are the very expensive, leather-backed type try putting them in a pillow case in the washing machine on a coolish wash, they take some time to dry afterwards so you will need a duplicate set of brushes, but they will be clean.

Fodder and Feed

Food hygiene is extremely important and to prevent contamination by rat and mouse faeces all feed must be stored in vermin-proof containers. Black plastic refuse bins with lids make good storage containers for concentrates and are less expensive than purpose made corn bins. Hay should be stored in a dry place where dogs and cats cannot get at it to foul it.

Feed and Water Containers

There is however, very little point in keeping the food clean if you are feeding it out of dirty buckets. Feed buckets should be washed out each time they are used in the same way as you do your own dinner plate.

Other receptacles that are also conveniently and frequently ignored are water buckets and troughs. It would be impractical to wash out a trough every day but a water bucket should certainly be scrubbed out daily to prevent the build up of slime. Troughs and automatic drinkers should be regularly inspected and cleaned to ensure the water is fresh and not stagnant.

Paddock Hygiene

Field hygiene is just as important as stable hygiene if you want to keep your horse free from parasites and provide them with a sweet bite to eat. If your paddock is on the small size it is absolutely essential that you pick up droppings on a daily basis. Horses will not graze where there are droppings, allowing the more aggressive pasture weeds such as dock to grow unchecked. Over-grazed pastures, where droppings are not picked up pose a very real risk as far as re-infection with endoparasites (intestinal worms) is concerned and a high worm burden will show in the quality of the coat and condition of the skin.

Muddy conditions around water troughs in summer provide an ideal breeding ground for a number of species of nuisance and biting flies, including the culicoides midge responsible for sweet itch, and in winter can lead to conditions which predispose mud fever.

Cleaning your horse's legs is very important but the manner in which you do this can make the difference between healthy skin and unhealthy skin. If your horse comes in from the field or from exercise with muddy legs, it is

A good example of a clean water trough area, shared between two horses in separate paddocks.

better to either allow the legs to dry and then brush the mud off or wash the legs with *cold* water before drying them thoroughly. Never wash muddy legs with warm water, however cold it is, as this will soften the skin and facilitate the entry of the bacteria that causes mud fever.

Tack

Keeping your tack clean does not take very long and will ensure that there is nothing to abrade or damage your horse's skin when we use it. Get into the habit of wiping it down with a damp cloth each time you use it to prevent the build up of dirt and grease and always wash the bit after it has been in the horse's mouth. Once a week strip your tack down (disassemble it) and check all the stitching, then clean and treat the leather with saddle soap. Be particularly vigilant with the girth as a dirty girth can cause a lot of problems.

Cleaning a bridle

For this you will need sponges, clean soft cloths, a nail brush, saddle soap, a couple of match sticks, metal polish and a bucket of warm water.

The first thing you need to do is strip the bridle down, this means undoing all the studs and buckles and taking it completely apart. If you are not used to doing this make a note of the number of holes each buckle is fastened on so that when you have put it back together, the bridle will fit the horse when you come to use it again, this is of course assuming it fitted in the first place. Having taken the bridle apart, drop the bit in the bucket of water and with a damp sponge clean all the dirt and grease from each piece of the bridle. You will notice that the leather has a smooth surface on one side with a rougher surface on the other. The rough surface is the inside and is the bit that rests next to the horse's skin, it is this surface that will pick up most of the grease. Make sure you remove all the dirt from the parts of the bridle that fasten round the bit rings like the reins and cheek pieces. Set the bridle pieces aside to dry.

Next apply the saddle soap to both sides of the bridle pieces, following the directions on the packaging and using a clean damp sponge. Make sure you work it well into the leather. Clean the buckles and studs with the metal polish and buff up and when the leather is completely dry polish the smooth side of the bridle with a soft clean cloth. Next scrub all the dirt from the bit and polish, making sure you wash the mouthpiece well to remove all traces of metal cleaner as no horse wants that nasty taste in his mouth. The bridle can now be put back together, remember 'studs on the inside buckles on the outside,' but before you do that, use the matchsticks to poke all the excess saddle soap out of the buckle and stud holes. Reassemble the bridle and put it away ready for use.

Cleaning a saddle

Strip the saddle down by removing the girth and the stirrup leathers and irons. If the irons have rubber treads take these out and drop the irons and the treads into a bucket of water to soak off any mud and dirt. Clean the saddle using a damp sponge taking care not to make it too wet and once it has dried apply the saddle soap. Be sparing with the soap on the seat and the flaps as you don't want these to become too soft, clean all the metal fittings and lightly oil the quick release mechanism on the stirrup bars. Once the saddle has dried rub over the outside surface with a clean dry cloth. The way you clean the girth will depend on what type of girth you have, if you have a leather girth the softer it is the better, fabric girths will need to be washed and the soft synthetic girths must have all the mud and grime removed before being used again. Clean the stirrup leathers and irons, scrub the treads and finally reassemble the saddle ready for use.

Other items of tack

All leather items of tack like martingales and breastplates, can be cleaned with water and saddle soap in the same way as the bridle. Numnahs should be regularly washed to remove any build up of sweat and dirt that might cause rubs under the saddle. If you use boots on your horse make sure these are also clean as they can, very quickly, do quite a lot of damage to the skin on your horse's legs.

Believe it or not some owners think nothing of using boots in this filthy condition. The dirt on the inside of this boot will act like sandpaper on the horse's leg.

The same boot as shown in the previous photograph, seen here from the outside. Just as dirty and worn.

These boots are not new or expensive but they have been cared for properly.

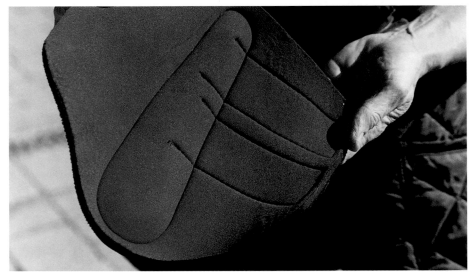

Setting yourself a routine for cleaning tack helps to save time and clean tack is much more comfortable for your horse to wear. In the long run it will save your horse's skin.

Cleaning the Genitals

Horse's genitalia need cleaning regularly and most people are familiar with cleaning the dock, and the vulva in mares as part of the normal grooming routine, however regular attention should also be paid to the sheath in geldings and stallions and the udder in mares.

As horses can be sensitive in this area, you need to take care not to get kicked, mares are easier to deal with as it is a relatively simple procedure to wipe down the udder using baby wipes, geldings and stallions take a bit more effort. It has been my experience that some horses get dirtier than others and in fact I know a vet who maintains a gelding's sheath is self-cleaning and does not require attention, I'm not sure I am fully in agreement with him. However, my own horses don't seem to get dirty at all, but it is a good idea to get the horse used to being handled in this area.

A horse's sheath is made up of lots of folds of skin with the penis retracted up inside it. The whole apparatus is lubricated by excretions called smegma which trap bits of dirt and debris and can get quite crusty. When the horse has a really dirty sheath a discharge will be evident down the back legs and this in turn will attract flies.

Some horses make a great fuss about sheath cleaning so you will need to approach the job with a great deal of sensitivity. If he is very dirty you may need to loosen the dirt and crust over several days before sluicing the sheath out. To soften the dirt you can use baby oil but I prefer to use grapeseed or sweet almond massage oil as it is vegetable and not mineral based, leave it on for a day then sponge off with warm water. It is entirely down to the individual horse how often this needs to be done.

The First Aid Kit

First aid kits are essential in the stable and for travelling with and commercial kits are available from places selling equine equipment. It is no use having a well stocked kit in the tack room back at the stable yard if you don't have one with you with you when travelling and are most likely to need it. One other thing, don't forget yourself – either make sure your kit contains all the things you might need yourself or have a separate first aid kit.

For treatment and cleaning of the skin your kit should contain the following, other items can be added according to your own preference and the needs of your horse.

- Hibiscrub

- Surgical spirit

- A clean bucket

- Bandages and vet wrap

- Sterile syringes and needles – for irrigation of wounds

- Antiseptic cream

- Poultice

- Salt

- Iodine

- Waterproof plasters and tape

- Gamgee tissue

- Wound powder

- Antiseptic disinfectant

- Vaseline

- Antiseptic spray

- Fly spray

- Melolin dressings

- 'Ice' pack

- Bot knife

- Cotton wool

- Clean towels

- Antiseptic wipes.

Extras could include:

- Essential oils: tea tree, eucalyptus, lavender, citronella, thyme

- Aloe vera gel

- Spray bottle

When to Call the Vet

Following an injury always call the vet if:

- There is profuse bleeding.

- There is any risk of the horse going into shock.

- If the horse is very lame.

- There is any kind of contamination or there could be a foreign body in the wound.

- Vital structures such as joints or tendon sheaths are involved.

- The wound needs stitching or is more than a couple of inches long. Large deep injuries or wounds that gape will probably need stitching. Maximum benefit will be gained from stitching if it is done as quickly after the injury as possible. Left open for over twelve hours and the wound is likely to be infected. Tissue at the edges will have deteriorated and in all probability will not hold a stitch.

- The wound is a deep puncture.

- The horse has not been vaccinated for tetanus.

- You are in any doubt what so ever.

First Aid – What to Do

The most important thing about your first aid kit is that you should know how to use it. First aid should be exactly what it says it is – the first thing you do to aid the situation. It is no use dithering about: learn the basics of effective first aid and apply them appropriately, confidently and promptly to either injured horse or rider.

Different circumstances require different actions, for instance you wouldn't treat a horse with a puncture wound for an allergic reaction. As with any kind of first aid the very first thing you must do is to assess the situation in terms of safety. Do not put yourself at risk. Secondly, don't panic, calmness will enable you to keep the situation under control.

The most common conditions requiring first aid are wounds but any kind of injury will require you to:

1. Prevent further injury. If you are able move the horse to a safe place.

2. Control bleeding by applying a clean dry pad to the wound for about five minutes when clotting should be underway.

3. Prevent open wounds from becoming contaminated with dirt and grit.

4. Minimize the risk of infection by gentle cleaning.

And What Not to Do

There are a number of 'no nos' to be aware of when administering first aid.

- Don't use cotton wool as this can contaminate the wound.

- Don't use strong antiseptics as they can damage delicate tissue as well as killing bacteria. Use salt solution to clean wounds.

- Don't use artificial spray on skin, it will seal in bacteria.

- Don't use any pressure as again this can damage delicate tissues and structures. If you are using a hose to flush out a wound only allow it to trickle over the injury.

- Don't wait before calling the vet if you need one.

- Don't use dirty bandages to cover wounds.

- Don't poke about in a wound as you will introduce bacteria and make the situation worse.

Shock

Shock is a very serious condition for a horse and one that requires immediate veterinary attention. It can be brought on by a number of circumstances such as trauma, dehydration and fluid loss, pain and infection. Circumstances leading to injury and associated with severe fright can easily trigger shock as can a serious bout of colic.

The mechanics of shock are the same regardless of whether it is you or your horse. The body responds by shutting down the circulatory system which starves the tissues and organs of oxygen. The end result is failure of the major organs and ultimately death.

Symptoms of shock are quite easy to spot. The horse's breathing will be rapid and he may be shivering or shaking, his pulse will be weak and the mucous membranes will be pale and may take on a bluish colour, this is an indication of circulatory failure and consequent lack of oxygen to the tissues. As the circulation shuts down the extremities, for example the ears, will feel cold.

If you think your horse may be going into shock, do not wait, call a vet *immediately*. Keep the horse calm and rug him up if he is showing signs of being

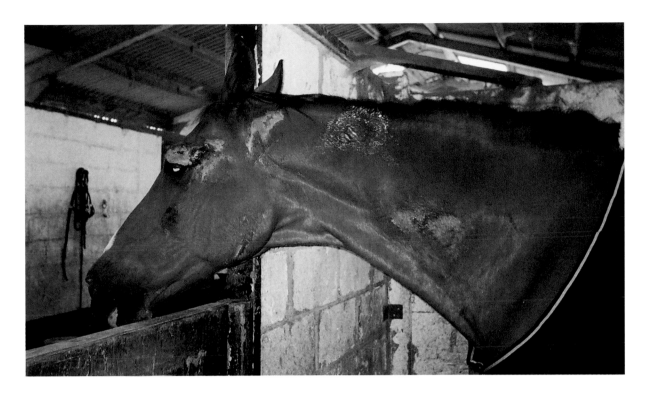

cold but don't allow him to overheat. There should be a good supply of clean water available just in case he is dehydrated. Once the vet is on his way you can deal with any other injuries. On arrival the vet will want to ascertain the cause of the shock, and having done this will take appropriate action, treatment for shock usually involves administering fluids, possibly with an electrolyte to replace lost salts. Antibiotics may be given for any infection. If the horse is bleeding and you have not already dealt with it, it will need to be stopped.

If a horse is unable to drink he will probably need to be hospitalized to administer sufficient quantities of fluid (40 to 80 litres per day) intravenously.

Cuts and Abrasions

Any kind of breach in the integrity of the skin should be dealt with as soon as possible to minimize the risk of infection. All wounds, no matter how small must be cleaned and you may need to do this before making the decision to call a vet. A little blood goes a very long way and things may not be as bad as they originally looked once the area has been swabbed. This can be done with a swab and warm salt solution working without applying any pressure from the middle of the wound towards the edges. This will help prevent pushing any dirt in the wound further in but if after cleaning you can still see dirt in there a trickle of water from the hosepipe frequently does the job.

Overnight this horse became cast in his box and had obviously been down for some time when breakfast time came round. In order to get him out and up on his feet the Fire Brigade were called to demolish the stable around him. Sensibly the vet was called immediately he was discovered and was able to treat him successfully for shock as well as multiple contusions. In this photograph his injuries are about a week old.

Once the wound has been cleaned you will be in a better position to assess whether or not you should call the vet. Minor cuts and grazes can be dusted with wound powder but if you are going to call the vet it is best not to apply any medicaments until he has inspected the injury. More serious injuries should be covered with a lint free dressing held in place with a bandage, all dressings will need changing twice a day until a scab has formed and if a wound has become infected it may be necessary to poultice it to draw out the infection.

Puncture Wounds

Puncture wounds can be extremely serious and most times the first indications you have that there is a problem are heat and swelling from infection that has already set in. Spotting puncture wounds before they become a problem requires vigilance. They are usually indicated by a slight swelling and a small trickle of blood, indicating the skin has been breached. Clip the hair away from the area but avoid putting any pressure on the wound as this may drive any foreign bodies or dirt further in. If there is infection you may need to poultice the area to draw it and any foreign bodies out, but you should call the vet as the horse may need a course of antibiotics to kill the bacteria. It is vital that the horse is covered for tetanus.

Leg Wounds

In order to assess the damage clip the hair (with scissors not clippers) from around the wound itself, if there is bleeding apply a sterile pad to stop it. As with all wounds it needs to be cleaned and this is probably best done with a low pressure hose. If the wound is anywhere near a joint or tendons call the vet as infection in either of these is a serious matter and can have catastrophic consequences.

Overreach, Speedicut, Strike Injury and Treads

As we have seen in an earlier chapter an overreach is when the hind foot strikes into the heel of the fore. A wound caused by the hoof striking the inside of the opposite leg, front or back, either below the knee or the hock is known as a speedicut whilst a strike injury occurs when the hind foot hits the front leg above the heel. Treads are wounds round the coronet caused by the horse standing on himself, they frequently happen when travelling.

All of these injuries can be very minor scrapes and scratches but they can also be serious enough to affect the horse's working potential so the correct first aid is very important. However, regardless of how superficial the wound may seem, if the horse is very lame, call the vet.

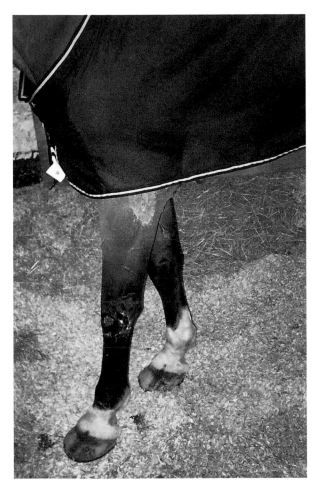
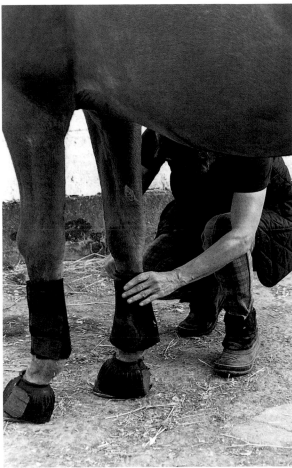

Most horses with these kinds of traumatic wounds will show a degree of lameness as the leg will undoubtedly be sore and there will be bruising, if the lameness persists, again you need to call the vet as it is usually an indication of something more serious going on.

Stop any bleeding by applying a clean pad to encourage clotting, once this has stopped, clean the wound by either gently swabbing with warm salt water or use a hose on low pressure. With this latter treatment the cold water has the added advantage of numbing the area and thereby easing pain.

Once you are able to see the damage you will be able to assess it better but remember, in the areas that these injuries happen, it is all too easy to damage important structures. Look out for deep wounds that may compromise the tendon sheath and wounds to the back of the cannon bone that could mean the tendons have been damaged. With coronary band injuries, suspect damage to the coffin joint.

Finally, having cleaned the wound, cover it with a healing gel, and secure a dressing place.

above left Leg injury over a joint sustained when the horse became cast in his box. At this point the injury was a week old.

above right Fitting boots on an old horse to protect his legs when out in the field. The overreach boots are very low at the back but a smaller size may chaff the pastern. It might be possible to trim these down a bit to accommodate this horse's rather shallow feet.

Rashes

Allergic reactions, urticaria, can look very alarming but in most cases they resolve themselves within a few hours. The lesions can develop very rapidly and can disappear just as quickly without treatment so the most sensible first aid you can apply is to try to reduce any itchiness with calamine lotion or, if the area is not too large, cool compresses. It might also help to bring the horse into the stable whilst you try to ascertain the cause of the reaction. If the condition does persist you should call the vet who may then prescribe steroids.

Swellings

Swellings can be something and nothing, from a simple fly bite to an abscess and you will need to decide what it is before you can treat it effectively. How the swelling is treated will also depend on where it is sited and how hot and painful it is to the touch. In some cases the horse may be obviously unwell.

Fly bites

Fly bites are conical in shape and usually have a hard centre with a softer outer area, the horse will probably not have any other symptoms although they may be tender and warm to the touch. The bites of some flies are very irritating and the horse may try to rub on anything convenient, he should be prevented from doing this as it can lead to infection setting in.

Hosing with cold water or applying an ice pack will help to relieve the symptoms a little but it is much better to prevent the problem in the first place by using plenty of good quality fly repellent and fly screen rugs and masks. If the bite is in the saddle area the horse should not be ridden until the swelling has gone down.

Abscesses

An abscess is a collection of pus and they are usually more round than fly bites and can be very painful indeed in the latter stages. They form in response to the introduction of a foreign body like a thorn although they frequently form at the sites of injections. Abscesses are not usually painful as they are forming but as they develop the pressure inside them builds up making them very sore and hot to touch.

Before any treatment is given the cause of the abscess must be ascertained and discussed with a vet. Strangles, which is an infectious disease of horses, presents with abscesses of the lymph nodes behind and beneath the lower jaw. This is a serious condition and stables where the disease occurs are usually quarantined.

Treatment of abscesses is with antibiotics and, if it is practical, poulticing to promote rupture and draw any foreign body out. Once it has burst the contents should be encouraged to drain completely, with daily bathing with a mild antiseptic until the swelling goes down and healing commences.

Fly strike

Fly strike occurs when an untreated open wound becomes contaminated by flies laying their eggs. The eggs then hatch into maggots that feed on the surrounding tissue, preventing effective healing and allowing the entry of bacteria. The wound must be thoroughly cleaned and all the maggots removed. Because flies carry such unpleasant bacteria it will probably be necessary to administer antibiotics.

Practical Treatment

There are a number of different ways of treating injuries but mostly these involve the application of either hot or cold agents. The condition itself will dictate what type of treatment you need to apply.

Poultice

A poultice or fomentation is a preparation of hot moist material applied to any part of the body to increase the circulation and draw noxious matter out, usually through a breach in the skin. They are frequently used for puncture wounds in the foot and for this a poultice boot is very useful for holding the poultice in place. There are a number of products on the market now, such as animalintex, which are used for poulticing and it is still possible to get kaolin, a type of clay. This, when prepared properly has the ability to retain heat for quite long periods of time.

To prepare a poultice the kaolin is heated, in its tin (without the lid), in a pan of boiling water, before being sandwiched in a spread between two layers of clean material. This is then applied to the affected area (the kaolin should not come in contact with the skin), covered with a dressing and secured in place by either tapes or bandages, care should be taken not to burn the skin by applying the poultice when it is too hot. It can be left in place for twelve hours.

An indication of the effectiveness of a poultice is the evidence of an unpleasant smelling discharge on the surface of the pad next to the area being treated. Treatment should continue until there is no sign of the discharge.

Animalintex and other products of the same ilk are probably easier to use as one has only to follow the directions on the packaging.

Tubbing

Again this is a type of fomentation used for wounds in the foot but tubbing would be used more to encourage existing drainage rather than to initially provoke it. If for some reason poulticing is not possible, it might help. Having once scrubbed it out, the horse is encouraged to stand with his foot in a bucket of hot water, not so hot as to be uncomfortable, for ten to fifteen minutes. The leg should be dried properly afterwards and a dressing applied to prevent further contamination of the wound. Tubbing would be done twice a day for three to four days.

Hosing

Cold water hosing is great for reducing inflammation and swelling and easing pain. Within reason it can be used anywhere but is mostly used for treating injuries to the legs. Hosing involves running a low pressure stream of cold water over the site of the injury being treated for about twenty minutes at a time. This treatment may need to be done every day for several days until the inflammation and swelling subsides. Start below the injury and gradually move upwards until the water runs over the affected area, legs should be done in pairs and should be dried well after hosing.

Nowadays it is possible to buy therapeutic boots which, when connected up to the hose, will reproduce the effect for you.

Ice Packs

There are a number of ways of applying cold to an area requiring treatment. These include bags of frozen peas, gel boots that can be put in the freezer and other items that can be bandaged on. With people the traditional treatment for sprains is RICE – rest, ice, compression and elevation. With horses the elevation bit is not possible but the rest, ice and compression can be applied to good effect.

10.

Complementary, Alternative and Other Therapies

There is no substitute for a qualified Veterinary Surgeon.

The Holistic Approach

In this more enlightened day and age it is only right and proper that we should be exploring more natural remedies than some of the aggressive and synthetic preparations used by conventional medicine. Don't get me wrong, it can and does work wonders and I would probably not be here writing this book if it were not for conventional medicine. We are all aware that some of the drugs used nowadays can have very unpleasant side-effects either in the short or long term, in other words, sometimes the cure can be worse than the disease. However, as a qualified therapist myself, both for humans and animals, it makes me very angry to hear some of the utter rubbish spouted by some people both in and out of the 'medical' profession at large.

According to the *Oxford Concise Medical Dictionary* the word 'holistic' is an adjective 'describing the approach to patient care in which the physical, mental and social factors in a patient's condition are taken into account rather than just the diagnosed disease'.

The big problem with conventional treatment is that it tends to target the condition and does not necessarily treat the whole being, either horse or human, in other words it is not holistic. Holistic medicine takes into consideration all the systems of the body not just a set of symptoms in isolation, often with excellent results where conventional, more modern medicine has failed. With the holistic approach, the body's own healing powers are stimulated into action greatly improving the chances of recovery. However there will always be some conditions and diseases which you will be fighting a losing battle against so don't run off with the notion that holistic treatments, conventional or otherwise, can cure all, they can't.

I have included this chapter to bring some understanding to this thorny subject although not all alternative or complementary therapies have any kind of intimate relationship with the skin, some do, and I have indicated these in the various sections, others have no relationship at all. However if we consider the skin to be the barometer of a horse's health anything which improves his physical or mental well-being will necessarily have a positive effect on the skin.

Alternative or Complementary

Over the past few years a booming industry has grown up, both for the treatment of people and animals, in what is generally and mistakenly called alternative therapies and because of a number of different factors, not least of all the legality of the situation it is very important that we understand the difference between 'alternative' and 'complementary' and apply the terms correctly to the various therapies themselves. It is also of equal importance that we consult only those with proper qualifications and insurance to practise any therapies we choose to employ.

The term 'alternative' implies 'instead of' or 'as a replacement for' whilst 'complementary' works more as an enhancement and goes alongside other therapies either conventional or not. For myself and my horses I prefer the holistic approach but having said that I am always guided by my doctor and my vet and, following consultation, on no account would I employ any therapies against their wishes.

In circumstances where more conventional treatments are having little or no effect on the disease, your vet will probably be quite open to trying other types of treatment as he is as interested as you are in getting your horse well again, but, you must discuss this with him and gain his permission first before taking any further course of action.

Homoeopathy

Homoeopathy is regarded more as an alternative to conventional medicine rather than a complementary therapy and in order to practise equine homoeopathy you need to be a qualified vet. Briefly homoeopathy is a branch of medicine which propounds that a substance which causes a range of symptoms can be used to treat any illness or condition that demonstrates the same set of symptoms. The more alike the symptoms caused by the substance and the symptoms of the disease are, the better the chance of successful treatment.

Homoeopathic medicines contain infinitesimally small amount of the substance being used in the treatment, so small in fact that it is impossible to detect them. Explanation of how they work is beyond the scope of this book, suffice it to say they do work for both people and animals although, because of the barrier in communications they tend to work better in people than in animals.

Homoeopathic vets are conventionally qualified vets who have received additional training in homoeopathy.

Herbal Medicine

Herbalism has its roots back in the mist of time and as herbivores, horses respond very well to treatment with medicinal herbs, frequently when conventional medicine has failed. Having gone out of fashion in the past few years it is now fortunately making a comeback with many horse owners recognizing the value of herbs in the horse's diet and the potency of herbs used as medicines. Some medicinal herbs when mixed together are not very palatable and in the old days these would be formed into a ball, possibly using some kind of fat, and blown into the back of the throat for the horse to swallow, it is unlikely that we would opt to employ such methods of delivery in this day and age, even if we had the appropriate equipment.

Herbs can be fed in their dried form and these will keep for a short time if they are properly dried, if you are going to have a go at this yourself do make sure you pick:

- Only that which you can positively identify.

- Herbs that have not been contaminated with exhaust fumes, herbicides or other toxins that may remain in the plant.

- Only plants that are not endangered species or protected in the wild.

If you do want to dry your own herbs for medicinal use it is much better to grow them yourself from seed supplied by a reputable seed merchant but be aware that the seed should only come from species plants and not from hybrids or cultivars.

There are a number of other methods of preparing herbs for medicinal use. Infusions are made by pouring boiling water over the soft parts of the plant such as the leaves and flowers, leaving to cool and straining off the liquor. Inhalations involve breathing the steam of an infusion and are an old remedy used to treat respiratory complaints whilst decoctions are made by grinding and boiling the woody parts of the plants to extract the active ingredients. Tinctures, made with dried plant material, are alcohol based and will keep for years.

Even though they are both plant based, herbal medicine and essential oil therapy are totally different to one another although both should be treated with caution.

Tissue Salts

Tissue salts should not be confused with electrolytic salts which are a totally different thing. In 1888 Dr Wilhelm Schussler published a book which is today called *Schussler's Twelve Tissue Remedies* and even after this long time it is still a standard work. There is however, no recorded data on the effect tissue salts have on horses but it is expected to be the same as that produced in humans.

There are twelve inorganic cell salts which comprise Schussler's remedies and he observed:

- Disease does not occur if cell metabolism is normal.

- Cell metabolism is in turn normal if cell nutrition is adequate.

- As far as the body is concerned nutritional substances are either organic or inorganic by nature.

- The ability of the body cells to assimilate, excrete and further to utilize nutritional material is impaired if there is a deficiency in the inorganic material.

Tissue salts are used with great success in both homoeopathy and biochemic therapeutics to treat a wide range of conditions and although they are perceived as providing food for cells this can hardly be the case as the doses are much too low for them to be classed as a nutritional supplement.

There is one more thing about tissue salts that should be noted, because they are naturally occurring within the body there is no way they can conflict with other medications or be taken in excess no mater how much is consumed. Tissue salts particularly relevant to the skin are:

3 Calc sulph (Calcium sulphate)	Skin healing
2 Calc phos (Calcium phosphate)	Itching
7 Kali sulph (Potassium sulphate)	Skin eruptions with scaling or sticky exudations. Also a skin conditioner.

9 Nat mur (Sodium Chloride)	Any kind of excessive dryness or moisture
12 Silica (silicon dioxide)	Brittle nails (hooves). Dull and life-less hair.

The twelve single tissue salts and eighteen combinations are available from good chemists and health stores

Essential Oil Therapy

Many people will be more familiar with this under the heading of aromatherapy but this is in fact an inaccurate description as it implies therapy through the sense of smell alone and ignores the fact that essential oils are frequently administered as treatments for specific conditions through the skin. It is also unfortunate that the word aromatherapy tends to conjure up visions of beauty salons providing a relaxing or rejuvenating half hour accompanied by various delightful odours.

It is very unfortunate that within recent years big business has jumped on the aromatherapy bandwagon in a big way and there are now literally hundreds of products, both for people and horses, that claim to be aromatherapy based. Some of these are very good whilst others are a downright con and sorting out which is which can be very difficult. However a little bit of tea tree oil in a shampoo or a few drops of citronella in a fly spray does not constitute Essential Oil Therapy.

Essential oils are very powerful extracts from various parts of plants. Oils can be extracted from flowers, leaves, twigs, roots, seeds and bark depending on the plant being used for the extraction, some plants have oils extracted from more than one part and these separate oils will have different names and natures. Without exception all essential oils are to some degree anti-microbial and, in fact, in laboratory tests thyme was found to be thirteen times more powerful than phenol for killing certain bacteria.

The efficacy of essential oils has long been recognized and before the advent of antibiotics they were extensively used in such places as hospitals to sterilize instruments and prevent the spread of airborne diseases. They are also excellent for the treatment of a number of skin conditions such as wounds, burns and ulcers which heal noticeably quicker than would normally be expected.

Because of their powerful nature essential oils should not be used on horses without first consulting a qualified practitioner, after consultation with your vet of course. It is illegal for any person other than a vet to administer any form of treatment to someone else's horses that they are not in control of. However, the value of an experienced and qualified practitioner lies in the fact that they can train you to use the oils and the fascinating thing about essential oils and horses is that they will, given the opportunity, select the correct oils that they need for themselves.

This all now begins to look a bit like magic and quackery but if you look at the properties of the oil the horse has chosen against the profile of the disease you will see that they are always right, however, if the oil properties and the disease profile do not match you may need to reassess the diagnosis and look more closely at what you are trying to treat the horse for.

For this reason horses should never, under any circumstances, be given any oil that they have rejected. Having offered the oil to the horse to smell a rejection can be as simple as turning the head away until the offending odour has been removed or as dramatic as rushing to the back of the stable, acceptance takes the form of licking, smelling with both nostrils, not turning away or continuous snuffling.

Some essential oils are extremely hazardous but from the point of view of treating the skin there are several that can be used quite safely undiluted for various minor conditions. Neat lavender is excellent for sunburn and as a counter irritant to fly bites, tea tree is very gentle at the same time as being anti viral and anti bacterial whilst yarrow is an anti-inflammatory. Other conditions that respond well to essential oils are sweet itch and mud fever and it is possible to make up an extremely effective fly repellent using a mixture of essential oils, aloe vera gel and water.

Essential oil therapy is a complementary therapy and not an alternative to conventional medicine. The oils can be administered through the skin by application in a carrier substance but are more usually absorbed through the mucous membranes of the tongue when licking the diluted oil. In my opinion it is essential that the therapist has a thorough knowledge of the properties and the chemistry of essential oils before attempting to use them, regrettably I have only met one vet who was suitably qualified in these prerequisites.

Bach Flower Remedies

Dr Edward Bach discovered that emotional states and types of people could be linked to specific attributes of certain plants. In all he developed thirty-eight single flower remedies and one combination, which he called Rescue Remedy specifically for calming and steadying the nerves in stressful situations.

Bach flower remedies are very safe to use but they do work and so you need to be ready for the consequences. For instance if you give your horse larch to build his confidence you may suddenly find yourself riding a much more forward going animal.

Bach flower remedies are administered in water and not applied to the skin but because they promote health and well-being there effects will indirectly show in the skin and the coat.

TTeam

An American woman named Linda Tellington-Jones has developed a training system consisting of a series of 'touches' and other exercises for use with horses which when used properly are very useful in overcoming any fears and reluctances a horse may have. It is therefore very useful for starting young horses and for retraining older horses that have had bad experiences and consequently developed bad habits. The principal of the system centres round a series of different movements, not unlike small massage movements, called touches and referred to as the Tellington Touch or by practitioners as the touch that teaches.

These light touches are worked all over the horse's body and consist of various arrangements of the hand and fingers making circular movements of exactly one and a quarter turns, either clockwise or anticlockwise, depending on which the horse prefers. In TTeam, the exact one and a quarter turns in the movement are very important, as this has been proven to activate all four types of brainwave, alpha, needed for the retention of information, delta, that are active in deep meditation, beta and theta. Apart from anything else the touches might do they are extremely relaxing and can calm a hyper horse in a very short space of time.

Acupuncture

Acupuncture is a therapy involving the insertion of fine needles through the skin at various points in order to balance the subtle energies and thus bring the body back to harmony and it is this disharmony that is believed to be the root cause of disease. In itself acupuncture is not thought of as a medical system but rather as an adjunct to either modern, western or traditional, Chinese medicine.

Energy or chi flows along meridians within the body and points along these meridians facilitate the alteration of the flow of chi. Because it is an invasive procedure only vets who are also qualified in acupuncture are legally allowed to practice.

Acupressure

This is a non-invasive therapy that works in the same way as acupuncture only without the needles. The practitioner works on the various points on the different meridians to balance the chi and by harmonizing the body reduces the state of 'dis-ease'. Pressure points along the meridians are activated by finger or thumb pressure in order to increase or reduce the chi depending on what is required.

The procedure starts with the 'opening' of the bladder meridian which runs from the ear, over the top of the head, down the neck, along the back, over the rump and down the back leg. To open a meridian you just draw a hand over it, in some cases you do not even have to touch the skin. This is followed by a flat hand exploration to locate any areas of heat, cold, tension or granulation, it is intimate with the skin and some horses take a while to get used to it. Once the

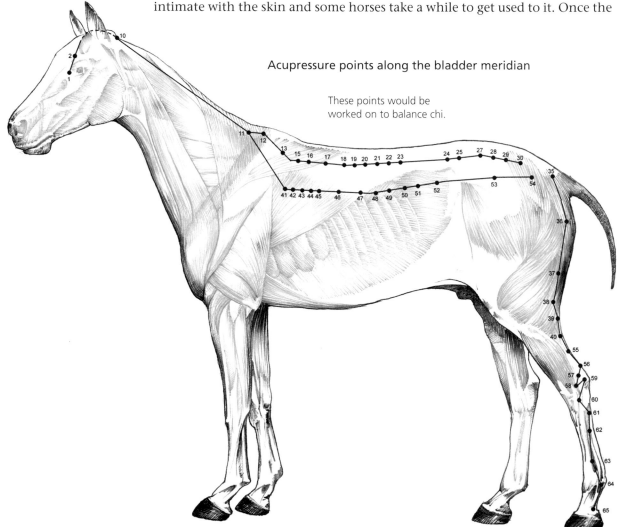

Acupressure points along the bladder meridian

These points would be worked on to balance chi.

points where the chi is 'stuck' have been located the practitioner will work on them to balance the chi and at the end of the session the meridians are closed down and the horse left to rest.

Therapeutic Massage

Nowadays the benefits of therapeutic massage are well documented and understood and you will find information on the techniques that can be used in the chapter on Maintenance of Healthy Skin. Used properly and on a regular basis it can have a profound and positive effect on well-being both physical and mental. Once again unless you propose to do this yourself you must find a reputable qualified practitioner, by now I know I am sounding like a cracked record but I do need to stress how important this is.

below left A chestnut on an eleven-year old horse. Chestnuts are as individual to horses as finger prints are to us.

If you are proposing to engage someone to give your horse a massage you must consult your vet first, most reputable practitioners won't carry out the procedure without the vet's consent anyway so you would be wasting your time if you don't get this permission. Massage can have quite a dramatic effect

below right A chestnut on a very old horse.

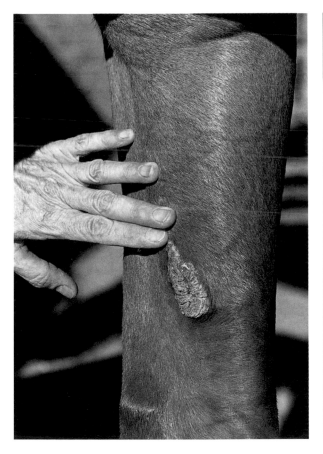

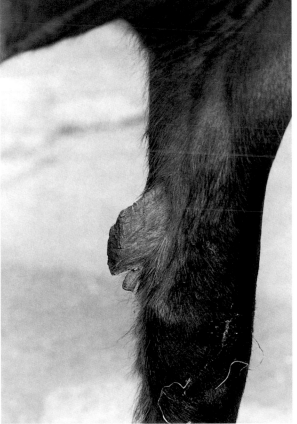

and may result in the horse behaving quite differently to the norm, especially if he has been suffering from stiff and sore muscles for quite a long time.

The object of the exercise is to loosen everything up so that the muscles are in a relaxed state ready for any work they may be asked to do but frequently they are in a state of tension causing a degree of discomfort or even pain if there is serious spasm. Releasing all of this will make the horse feel quite different both mentally and physically and this will inevitably have a knock on effect on his behaviour.

Needless to say massage works on the skin and the underlying structures and it may well be worth your while finding a practitioner who is qualified to do both you and your horse as you will be surprised at the difference having a massage yourself can make to your own riding position.

Kinesiology

Amongst other things this is an excellent diagnostic tool but when you first see kinesiology being used it looks like mumbo jumbo and it is very easy to discount the benefits it can bring. Kinesiology is basically muscle testing used to measure the energy flow throughout the body and to establish where weaknesses exist. Through a range of simple positions adopted by the person being tested various groups of muscle can be isolated and when gentle pressure is applied the strength or weakness of the muscles can be assessed.

Each muscle group relates specifically to an organ system in the body so that where there is a reduced flow of energy coming from an organ the muscle tests weak. The muscle groups and organ systems are linked by either a meridian or a lymph vessel so the connections are not quite as arbitrary as would first appear.

Muscle testing on horses is done through a surrogate either with their hand on the horse or with a piece of mane or tail hair. It is extremely good for establishing the cause of food or other allergies where it has not been possible to establish the cause of an allergic reaction and for locating the precise area of pain or injury, however you do need a competent practitioner and these are few and far between.

Because there is no treatment involved this is the one therapy where you can go ahead without consulting the vet first but be warned he will not like it if you suddenly start arguing about any diagnosis he has given. The situation calls for tact and discretion and in legal terms the vet is the only person allowed to make a proper diagnosis. There is however no reason why kinesiology cannot be used to check any diagnosis given.

Other Therapies

There are numerous other therapies of one persuasion to another. Copper bracelets are used in the same way as they are for people to help relieve the symptoms of arthritic pain and stiffness and electro-magnetic therapy which is where the electro-magnet is applied directly to the skin is used to promote healing and prevent muscle wastage.

One type of therapy that looks like being very beneficial is that given by the hydrotherapy spa. This consists of a unit, not unlike a very tiny stable with half height walls, which the horse walks into. Once the door is closed the unit fills with mineralized water that is continuously swirled round the legs for the length of the treatment. At the end of the treatment session the unit empties and the horse is led out.

There are of course many more therapies which I have not mentioned here as they have little relevance in a book on horses' skin but whatever treatments you choose for your horse remember the watch words *consult your vet first and make sure the therapist is properly trained and insured* you will not then go far wrong.

11.

Conclusion

Skin – the barometer to your horse's health.

If we have discovered nothing else on our journey here it is that if our horse's skin and coat are in dubious or poor condition then there is something wrong with the horse. In some cases we will not have far to look for the reason whilst in others tracking down the cause may take considerable time and effort, it is always worth taking the trouble.

Horses put up with a lot from us humans and even the most experienced and conscientious horseman won't get it right every time so don't be too hard on yourself when things occasionally go wrong. Life is a series of learning curves, some gentle some steep and we should not be too proud or conceited to learn from our experience or, in fact, from that of others at every opportunity offered.

At this point I need to tie up some loose ends and one of the things we have talked about is normal parameters which includes temperature, respiratory rate and pulse rate. Strictly speaking these have nothing to do with the skin but nevertheless, as I have alluded to them, I feel it necessary to include the information somewhere.

Taking a Horse's Temperature

The only effective way of taking a horse's temperature is with a thermometer in the rectum. Some thermometers are made especially for the purpose and if you have one all well and good. These can be inserted into the rectum and clipped onto the horse's tail so that the thermometer is not 'lost' during the process. If you don't have one of these don't worry, an ordinary shake down bulb thermometer is perfectly adequate but you will need to keep hold of it.

First shake the thermometer down so that the reading is below the level the temperature should be at. The horse will much prefer it if you warm the thermometer and lubricate it with Vaseline first. Hold the tail out of the way and insert the thermometer in the rectum with a twisting action. The thermometer needs to be inserted about two to three inches and should be held there for approximately three minutes. Remove the thermometer, wipe it clean and read the results. The normal temperature of an adult horse is between 37.5 and 37.8 degrees C or 99.5 and 100 degrees F. Foals have a slightly wide range which may go up to 38.9 C.

Taking the Pulse

A pulse can be felt at any point where a major artery is just beneath the skin but the most convenient place to take the pulse is where the external maxillary artery crosses over the lower border of the jawbone although it can also be taken on the inside of the knee. To take the pulse press lightly with the balls of the fingers until you can feel the thump, thump of the heart. When the horse is at rest there should be thirty-five to forty-five beats per minute.

Respiratory Rate

To take the rate of respiration you need to count the number of breaths per minute, (a breath being both in and out passage of air) by watching the rise and fall of the flanks or the movement of the nostrils. Viewing the horse from the rear and slightly to one side might help you as it can be difficult to see the movement of the flank. The average respiratory rate for a horse is between eight and fourteen breaths per minute.

What is Stress?

I have rattled on a good deal about stress and the effect it has on horses, particularly their skin, but up till now I have not attempted to quantify it. Stress is not something that can be accurately measured but a horse will be stressed if he needs to make abnormal or extreme adjustment in his normal behaviour pattern to be able to cope with his environment or the way he is dealt with. Stress is also a moveable feast in as much as what stresses him one day when he is feeling a bit under the weather may not stress him the day after when he has got over whatever it was that was troubling him, a bit like us really. Also to complicate matters further something that causes stress in one horse may not necessarily stress another, a couple of good examples of this would be travelling and being shod.

It is not possible to never stress our horses and indeed a certain level of challenge is good but there are certain stresses we should strive to avoid at all costs. These are:

- Poor nutrition

- Lack of water

- Neglect and bad management

- Lack of suitable company

- Bad housing and unsuitable or dirty conditions

- Badly fitting tack and equipment

- Unclear or confusing instructions

- Fear

- Inflicted pain

In my opinion none of the above are acceptable under any circumstances and with responsible, knowledgeable horse owners there is absolutely no excuse for any of them.

Types

To provide the right living conditions for our horses we need to understand a bit about the different types or breeds. The type or breed of a horse will dictate the job of work it is suitable for and the conditions and accommodation that is needed to keep it fit and healthy. The rules are very simple to follow but there will always be exceptions to them.

By and large, in winter horses with fine coats and thin skin such as Thoroughbreds need to be stabled at night and rugged up whilst grazing out in the field in the day, regardless of whether they are clipped or not although I know of an ex-racehorse that won't keep a rug on and doesn't like being in the stable at night, she is now twenty-eight years old and although she does look like an old horse she keeps her weight on very well with supplementary feeding and appears perfectly happy.

As a starting point you need to know what type bracket your horse falls into or, if you have not yet acquired one, what type of horse you are able to cope with and look after properly.

Thoroughbred

Thoroughbreds and Arabs are usually the most fine coated and thin skinned of all horses and although they can live out all year round, most do better and are more comfortable when brought in at night during the winter. In general they are thought of as hot blooded horses with temperaments to match, Thoroughbreds in particular are not really suitable for first time horse owners as they are more sensitive to the conditions they are kept in and the management they are subjected to. They are also much more nervy than crossbreds and are more unpredictable.

Thoroughbreds can be so fine skinned as to dislike anything but the very softest brushes being used when grooming and to use the average body or

Elegant lines of the Thoroughbred, fine limbs and lack of feather on the legs.

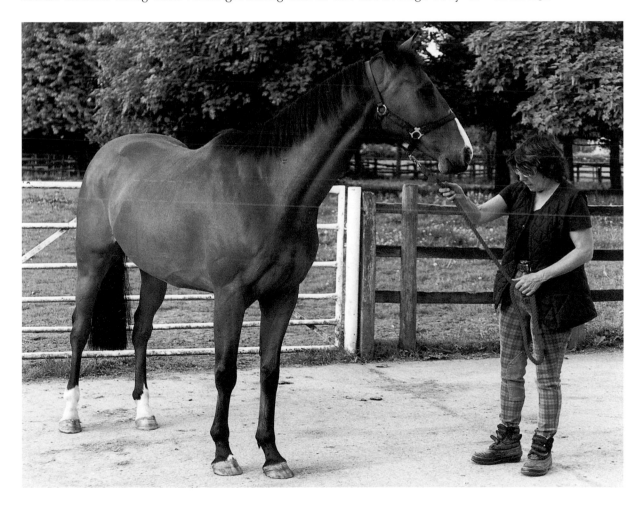

dandy brush is to court disaster. They are more prone to all kinds of diseases and can damage themselves more easily, they are in other word high maintenance horses.

I am aware that there are some people who will disagree with this statement and having made it, because of their intelligence, I have to say that I prefer the Thoroughbred to all other breeds of horses despite their drawbacks.

Warmblood

The term warmblood encompasses amongst others Hanoverians and Trakehners. These tend to be sturdier than Thoroughbreds and not so prone to life's little ills and they are also a good deal calmer if not downright lazy in their attitude to life. However they do tend to have quite fine coats and are better rugged in winter even if they are not clipped.

A typical British Hanoverian. Note the long back.

Native Pony

Native ponies, such as the Dartmoor, Exmoor and New Forest are at the other end of the scale to Thoroughbreds as are Shires and Haflingers. They sport very dense coats capable of protecting them from extremes of weather conditions in winter, this layer of insulation can be seen dramatically demonstrated by the Dartmoor ponies with unmelted snow on their backs. Native ponies do not need to be rugged up in winter, either in the stable or out of it, and in fact would be very uncomfortable if they were so.

And The Others

Most horses you come across are going to be crossbred and therefore a mixture of breeds so you will have to use your judgement about their type of skin and coat. This is not difficult to do once you are familiar and have been around horses for a little time but the one thing I must stress is that all horses are individuals and should be treated as such, even down to the weight of rug they wear. Inevitably there will be 'hot' Thoroughbreds and 'cold' natives so be aware of this and let the horse himself guide you.

Conclusion

Whatever you do, the health of your horse is dependent on the integrity of his skin and the health of the skin dependent on the good health of the horse in general. The two are inextricably interlinked. We already know that the skin, as the largest organ of the body, is involved in many vital functions and plays a huge role in the overall protection of the rest of the body as a whole: we ignore its needs at our peril, actually not *our* peril but that of our horse.

And...

Of course the real stars of this book are the horses who patiently put up with hours of photography, and varying degrees of prodding and pushing. Let me introduce you.

Ben

Ben is a twenty-four year old, 17hh, Belgian Warmblood gelding who has been with his current owner, Lorna, for the past fourteen years. Together they have done everything from cross-country to dressage and were still in the ribbons as recently as March 2004. In Lorna's words Ben has been 'the horse of a life-time'. A long term condition, a trapped nerve in his near hind, recently led to him becoming cast in his box and Lorna thought she was going to lose him. Happily he has now made a full recovery.

Goldie

Goldie is thirty-four years old and still looking good. Her present owner (Mary) rescued her, exhausted, twenty-four years ago from a riding school. Back then Goldie was very bad tempered and inclined to kick and nap but with patience, a proper diet and kind and gentle handling she turned out to be a versatile pony that many people have had lots of fun with. Having lived out nearly all her life Goldie now comes in at night.

Polo

Polo is a 16.1hh twenty-four year old shire cross Thoroughbred with a chequered history. His present owner, Alice, has had him thirteen years but prior to that, around seventeen years ago, Polo was a police horse. Unfortunately his career in the force was cut short and he was retired following a road accident.

Jabina

Jabina, at twenty-seven, although fit and well, is now retired. Bred by a palomino Arab stallion out of a chestnut Irish Draught mare, her early life was spent as a brood mare before she slipped twins and ended up in the local horse market. There she was bought by a local horse dealer and sold to her current owner, Janet. Several disastrous dressage outings led to the discovery of a trapped nerve in her groin so attention was turned to showing, something Jabina was good at, where she won many best condition and in-hand classes. Janet came back into riding in her forties and has had Jabina for sixteen years, she says 'Jabina has been a fantastic friend and a delight to look after. She has always been there for me and I feel privileged to have owned her'. Jabina is 16.1hh.

far left Ben with Lorna. His registered name is Bold Review.

left Goldie 14.3hh cob cross.

far left Polo, at twenty-four now going grey round his face.

left Jabina 16.1hh palomino.

Ted

17.1hh Warmblood who has been with his present owner, Charlotte, for the past three years. Ted has competed at affiliated level in both jumping and dressage and was used as a stallion up until the age of six when he was gelded. Ted is eleven years old.

Ryan

Seven years old and 16.1hh Thoroughbred cross by Carnival Drum. Ryan won the British Beginners show jumping at Bucks County Show prior to coming to his present owner, Gemma, in February 2004.

Smudge

Eight years old, 14.2hh has been with Shona for the past year. Smudge had previously been badly beaten and was mistreated as a youngster so she is quite wary, particularly of large, loud men and anybody with a whip. She now does

above Ryan.

top left Ted in action.

left Smudge.

all riding club activities. Smudge is a most unusual colour most resembling a very dark dun.

Mabel

British Hanoverian. Mabel arrived three years ago in a very poor condition with a serious liver problem from which she has now recovered. She had previously been a brood mare but was bred for dressage.

Duffy

Five years old, 15hh cob who will ride or drive. McDuff, Duffy for short, has a very high opinion of himself but is great fun to ride.

Solomon

15.3hh, Solomon had a very bad start in life from which he has never really recovered. He has been with me now for the past four years and is one of the most loving horses I have ever owned.

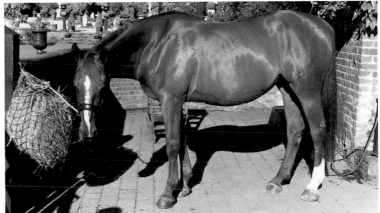

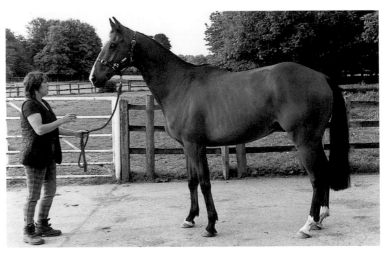

above right Mabel. Enjoying a snack between photo shoots.

above McDuff – known to us all as Duffy.

right Solomon. Not the most stylish horse but a lovely temperament.

Bee

Supremely elegant Bee, full name Miss Ellaneous, is thirteen years old and 15.2hh. Bee has been with her present owner, Michelle, for four years and they are always in the ribbons when competing. Bee is very fussy about who gets on her back, she just about tolerates the trainer, and has enough attitude and character for a whole yard full of horses.

Dermot

Dermot is a real gentleman and is probably in his mid twenties. In the past he has obviously had a hard life and a range of injuries at one time or another. However he still has his own ideas about when he should come in from the field and about how he should behave when being ridden, and that is more like a five year old.

Huck

Full name Huckleberry Finn. Huck is a 16.1hh chestnut Thoroughbred who is now twenty-eight years old. He is a real sweety and Carol, his owner has had him since he was five. During that time they have done everything together and still occasionally go for a plod round the roads – when Carol is feeling up to it!

below Miss Ellaneous.

below right Huck and Dermot out in the field.

'Thank goodness that's over with. What do you think she'll have us doing next?'

Acknowledgements

The author is grateful to the following for permission to reproduce copyright photographs in this book: **Julia Bradbury**, Chesham; **Christopher Thomas**, Viewlink Ltd, Chenies Parade, Little Chalfont, Amersham, Bucks HP7 9PY; **Equilibrium**, Unit 4, Upper Wingbury Farm, Leighton Road, Wingrave, Bucks HP22 4LW; **Shires Equestrian Products**; **Kate Negus Saddlery**, Old Abbey Barn, Bremhill, Calne, Wiltshire SN11 9HG; **Lavenham**, 24–25 Churchfield Road, Sudbury, Suffolk CO10 2YA; **Sue Devereux** (veterinary photographs).

The diagrams on pages 5, 17, 27, 35, 51, 90, 108, 192 are drawn by **Andrew Barton**, and those on pages 29 and 34 are drawn by **Rodney Paull**.

Special thanks also to Mr and Mrs T Bedford, Warren House, Chalfont St Giles, Bucks and to the horse owners and staff, Newhouse Farm Livery Stables, Chorleywood, Herts, for their help and cooperation.

Index